THE INDUSTRIAL ORGANIZATION OF THE GLOBAL ASSET MANAGEMENT BUSINESS

Ingo Walter

CFA Institute
Research
Foundation

Statement of Purpose

The CFA Institute Research Foundation is a not-for-profit organization established to promote the development and dissemination of relevant research for investment practitioners worldwide.

Cover Image Photo Credit: Guvendemir/Complicated Architecture/Getty Images

ISBN 978-1-934667-89-7

November 2015

Editorial Staff

Elizabeth Collins Editor	Cindy Maisannes Manager, Publications Technology and Production
Pat Light Assistant Editor	Christina Hampton Senior Publishing Technology Specialist

Biography

Ingo Walter holds the Seymour Milstein Chair in Finance, Corporate Governance and Ethics at the Stern School of Business at New York University (NYU). He has served as vice dean for academic affairs at NYU and as chair of the international business department and chair of the finance department. Professor Walter served as director of the NYU Salomon Center for the Study of Financial Institutions, director of the Stern Global Business Institute, and dean of the faculty at the Stern School of Business. He has had visiting professorial appointments at the Free University of Berlin, the University of Mannheim, the University of Zurich, the University of Basel, the Institute for South East Asian Studies, IESE Business School, the University of Western Australia, and various other academic and research institutions. He also held a joint appointment at INSEAD as professor of international management and remains a visiting professor there. Professor Walter has published papers in many professional journals in international economics and finance and has served as the author, co-author, or editor of 27 books. He has served as a consultant to various corporations, banks, government agencies, and international institutions and has held a number of board memberships. Professor Walter holds AB and MS degrees from Lehigh University and a PhD from NYU.

Acknowledgments

Many people who work in global funds management seek a better understanding of their own industry. It is diverse geographically and functionally, complex in structure and governance, and highly uneven in the availability of data sufficiently reliable for drawing meaningful conclusions. The good news is that there is plenty of expertise at the ground level involving disciplines ranging from actuarial science and asset allocation to risk management and sales and distribution.

Consequently, parts of this study at the sector level are built on discussions led by Stephen Brown, Martin Gruber, and Massimo Massa during a series of workshops hosted by SimCorp in Copenhagen, Denmark. These workshops succeeded in drawing on the expertise of industry practitioners and regulators to bolster the industrial organization models common in academia. Thanks are due Anthony Neuberger, Marc van den Berg, Arne E. Jørgensen, Jacob Elsborg, Annukka Paloheimo, and Frank Wellhöfer in the pension fund discussions; Ulrik Modigh, Brian S. Jensen, Peter Hertel, Bernard Delbecque, and Merele A. May in the discussion of mutual funds; and Marno Verbeek, Lester Gray, Michael Jarzabek, Lars Eigen Møller, Matthäus Den Otter, Ralf Schmücker, Peter Engel, and Dushyant Shahrawat in the debates on alternative assets.

Finally, the author gratefully acknowledges financial assistance from the CFA Institute Research Foundation.

Contents

Foreword

Over the past decade, few industries have experienced as much turmoil as the global asset management industry. The industry's prominence causes it to be a highly scrutinized segment of the financial services sector. As a business, asset management is huge, complex, and ever changing. For all of these reasons, the structure and characteristics of the global asset management industry are rarely studied, and for these same reasons, they must be—which is what Ingo Walter has done.

We usually turn our lens on some aspect of the financial scene, but in this book, the lens is turned around to look at ourselves. *The Industrial Organization of the Global Asset Management Business* provides practitioners with essential information on the current state of the investment management industry. It is an especially useful guide for students and others entering the field.

As Walter writes, "Many people who work in global funds management seek a better understanding of their own industry. It is diverse geographically and functionally, complex in its structure and governance, and highly uneven in the availability of data sufficiently reliable for drawing meaningful conclusions."

Walter's reflective study of global asset management provides the information that we, as professionals, need to make smart, informed business decisions; to effectively serve our clients; and successfully navigate the storms we will inevitably encounter in our future.

Walter starts with an overview of the asset management industry's architecture, then addresses the dynamics of each of its key sectors, including pension funds, mutual funds, hedge funds, private equity funds, and private wealth management. Through a straightforward, meticulous narrative, he looks at the history of each of these sectors, the challenges met during and after the global economic crisis of 2007–2009, cost and risk factors, opportunities for growth, and the ways in which each sector is poised to meet the next chapter in its history.

Walter describes the complexity of each of these sectors by product, business model, and global reach of the industry. His analysis of the pension fund sector is particularly strong. He identifies how our aging global population and the shift to a defined-contribution model of retirement savings are key game changers. He speaks of the need to broaden investment options for investors and to keep an eye on long-term outcomes, not simply the period-to-period performance of benchmarks. Walter also shows the profitability and scale of the business and hence its attractiveness to competition and to young people seeking a long and rewarding career. Concluding with a debate about asset management firms and their potential to incur systemic risk regulation, he suggests that this conversation is far from over.

The financial services industry is still feeling the effects of the global financial crisis, and in its aftermath, many industry characteristics have changed—particularly in the asset management industry. Walter writes, "As we now know, major financial shocks can no longer be contained. They spread with amazing speed, both geographically and across asset classes and financial intermediaries. Financial interconnectedness can bring great benefits, but it also generates large systemic risks, and few places provide refuge from its consequences."

Asset managers are living in a new world. We are still on the rebound, still struggling to regain investor trust, and our only sound strategy for a complete recovery is to rebuild the industry in a smarter, more sustainable way. Walter stresses the fiduciary nature of our business—hence, the need for a professional class to serve the industry. Through lessons learned, we know the asset management industry is globally connected and our collective action can have tremendous influence.

With this concept as a catalyst, CFA Institute has made it a top priority to work with the entire investment community to build a stronger, more trustworthy investment management profession and, ultimately, a better market for investors. How? Simply by putting investors first. As asset managers, our primary duty is to protect investor interests at all times. It is our responsibility to help build a sustainable industry through higher standards of professionalism at both an individual and a corporate level. In particular, we need higher standards for entry into the investment management profession because today in most countries, it is simply too easy to enter the business and claim competency to manage portfolios.

The prediction is that by 2025, a billion new middle-class consumers will emerge globally, which will represent the largest single-decade increase of potential clients in history. Global investable assets are expected to increase to more than $100 trillion by 2020. According to Walter, "The asset management industry is likely to be one of the largest and most dynamic segments of the global financial services industry in the years ahead. . . . Not only is this already massive industry likely to grow faster than other parts of the financial services sector, but also cross-border volume—both regional and global—is likely to take an increasing share of that activity."

Investors need the knowledge and expertise of trustworthy investment professionals now more than ever, and they need the assurance that the industry has their best interests in mind. The timing of Walter's book is impeccable;

it provides asset managers with a concise, yet all-encompassing, perspective on the global asset management industry.

Through Walter's fluent teaching, readers will come away with a firm understanding of this dynamic, complex, and ever-evolving industry. And although *The Industrial Organization of the Global Asset Management Business* provides invaluable insight into the ins and outs of the industry and all its components, its real value lies not in this information itself but in how readers can apply it for the greater good of their clients and society as a whole.

Paul Smith, CFA
President and CEO, CFA Institute
November 2015

1. Introduction

This study considers the industrial organization (IO) of the modern global asset management industry in terms of its structure, conduct, and performance, as is standard in the IO field. It provides a global perspective that reflects both the global nature of asset allocation decisions and the size and growth of the markets for fiduciary services in each of the major asset management markets.

Developed countries, represented by OECD markets, continue to be dominant in assets under management.[1] The fastest growth, however, lies elsewhere: Established players and new entrants are increasingly found in emerging-market countries. Because of this rapid change, market access and regulatory dynamics are among the key drivers of market definition and business strategies in the global asset management industry.

The industry is anything but simple. Asset owners include pension funds, endowed institutions, sovereign wealth funds, and individuals. The managers of the assets include investment management firms, insurance companies, mutual funds, and alternative asset managers (e.g., hedge funds and private equity firms).

The dynamics of the asset management business are both complex and geographically diverse. Products and vendors compete within and across clients and markets and often shade into each other. Regulation can differ dramatically among financial systems and functions, even when the objectives are the same: efficiency, growth, and stability on the "buy side" of the financial architecture.[2]

Such differences are amplified by the fact that industry data range from excellent to nonexistent. Yet the industry is expected to continue to grow at an impressive pace. As assets accumulate, they will inevitably be invested. The money has to go somewhere. The question is, where and how? What are the implications for growth, costs, and risks facing firms that compete in the business of asset management?

The asset management industry is likely to be one of the largest and most dynamic segments of the global financial services industry in the years ahead.

---

[1]The OECD (Organisation for Economic Co-Operation and Development) consists of 34 countries, mostly with advanced economies.

[2]Traditionally, the "buy side" refers to investment managers building portfolios on behalf of their clients (or with their own money) and the "sell side" refers to the broker/dealers and investment bankers who help corporations, governments, and others issue those securities. This distinction is not rigid, and the two sides shade into each other.

As of December 2014, the global total of assets under management (AUM) was estimated at close to US$74 trillion, which includes pension fund assets, funds managed by the insurance industry, mutual fund assets, alternative investment vehicles, and private wealth management but excludes sovereign wealth funds and external reserves of central banks.[3] Not only is this already massive industry expected to grow faster than other parts of the financial services sector, but also cross-border volume—both regional and global—is likely to take an increasing share of that activity.

Within this high-growth context, asset management attracts competitors from an extraordinarily broad range of strategic groups: commercial and universal banks, investment banks, trust companies, insurance companies, private banks, captive and independent pension fund managers, mutual fund firms, and various types of specialist firms. This rich array of contenders— marked by different starting points, skill sets, competitive resources, and strategic objectives—is likely to render the asset management market highly competitive, even though one can foresee a certain amount of consolidation.

This book provides an overview of the global institutional asset management industry. It includes a discussion of the competitive structure, conduct, and performance of the asset management industry and an assessment of the impact of institutional asset management on global capital markets.

---

[3]These amounts may involve some double counting—for example, if some of the assets of a private wealth client are invested in mutual funds. In addition, some assets have almost certainly been omitted from this counting. Source: Boston Consulting Group (2015) asset management survey at https://www.bcgperspectives.com/content/articles/financial-institutions-global-asset-management-2015-sparking-growth-through-go-to-market-strategy/.

2. Asset Management in a Financial Intermediation Framework

Asset management services—the buy side of global financial markets—are depicted in **Figure 1**.

Pension funds take two principal forms: (1) those guaranteeing a level of benefits to participants and (2) those that build savings balances owned by participants individually, from which retirement income will be drawn. The first kind—called "defined-benefit (DB) pension funds" in many jurisdictions, including the United States—may buy securities directly in the market or place funds with banks, trust companies, or other types of asset managers. In this process, they are often aided by fund consultants who advise pension trustees on performance and asset allocation styles. The second kind, called "defined-contribution (DC) pension plans" or "DC savings programs," offers mutual funds and other securities for participants to buy with their own money, to which a company (sponsor) match may or may not be added.

Foundations, endowments, and financial reserves held by nonfinancial companies, institutions, and governments can rely on in-house investment expertise to purchase securities directly from the institutional sales desks

Figure 1. The Asset Management Architecture

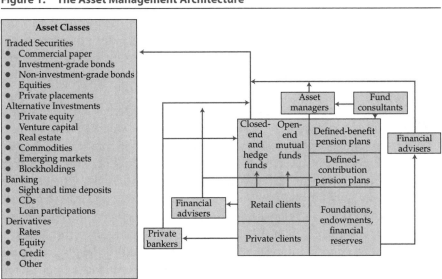

Note: CD here refers to "certificate of deposit."

of banks or securities broker/dealers. They can use financial advisers to help them build portfolios or place funds with institutional asset management firms, alternative asset managers, and open-end or closed-end mutual funds.

Retail clients have the option of placing funds directly with financial institutions, such as banks, or purchasing securities from the retail sales representatives of broker/dealers, possibly with the help of fee-based financial advisers. Alternatively, retail investors can choose to have their funds professionally managed by buying shares in mutual funds or unit trusts (again, possibly with the help of advisers), which, in turn, buy securities from the institutional sales desks of broker/dealers (and, from time to time, maintain balances with banks).

"Private" (i.e., wealthy) clients are broken out as a separate segment of the asset management market in Figure 1. They are usually serviced by private bankers who bundle asset management with various other activities, such as tax planning, estate planning, and trust services. They place assets directly into financial instruments, commingled managed-asset pools, and sometimes mutual funds and unit trusts. The upper end of the wealth management spectrum includes services provided by both single-family and multifamily offices.

The estimated size and composition of global financial markets are depicted in **Table 1**, which includes equities and fixed-income instruments issued by governmental and private sector entities (including securitizations). These categories make up the "raw material" of the asset management industry, which in its fiduciary capacity, holds the vast bulk of these claims and ownership rights. Note the size and character of the impact of the 2007–08 global financial crisis and the recession that followed in terms of the immediate decline in asset values and apparently longer-term decline in global asset growth.

With the passing of the financial turbulence, many things have changed for global finance, particularly the asset management industry. As we now know, major financial shocks can no longer be contained. They spread with amazing speed, both geographically and across asset classes and financial intermediaries. Financial interconnectedness can bring great benefits, but it also generates large systemic risks, and few places provide refuge from its consequences. Nor is the real economy spared. The global aftereffects of the deepest and longest recession since the 1930s are still (almost a decade after the Lehman Brothers collapse that, arguably, defined the peak of the crisis) reflected in sluggish economic growth in many developed countries, delayed capital expenditures, persistently high unemployment, and intractable fiscal deficits among countries in Europe and among states and municipalities elsewhere.

Table 1. Global Stock of Debt and Equity Outstanding (US$ trillions except as noted, end of period, constant 2010 exchange rates)

Sector	1990	1995	2000	2005	2006	2007	2008	2009	2010	Compound Annual Growth Rate	
										1990–1999	2009–2010
Nonsecuritized loans outstanding	22	24	31	38	40	43	45	47	49	4.1%	5.9%
Securitized loans outstanding	2	3	6	11	14	15	16	16	15	12.7	–5.6
Nonfinancial corporate bonds outstanding	3	3	5	6	7	8	8	9	10	6.7	9.7
Financial institution bonds outstanding	8	11	19	29	35	41	41	44	42	9.5	–3.3
Public debt securities outstanding	9	13	16	25	28	30	32	37	41	7.8	11.9
Stock market capitalization	11	17	36	45	55	65	34	48	54	8.1	11.8
Total	54	72	114	155	179	202	175	201	212	7.2	5.6
Financial depth (%)[a]	261	263	321	334	360	376	309	356	356		

[a]Calculated as global debt and equity outstanding divided by global GDP.

Note: Numbers may not sum because of rounding.

Sources: Bank for International Settlements, Dealogic, Securities Industry and Financial Markets Association, Standard & Poor's, McKinsey Global Banking Pools, and McKinsey Global Institute analysis.

As expected, the asset management industry has not been spared. Massive losses starting in 2007 affected the size of assets managed by almost all fund managers except for a few hedge funds that correctly bet against the asset classes that declined. As we now know, banks were heavily exposed to the toxic assets they were intermediating because, as investors, they had assumed "warehousing risk" in addition to their "pipeline risk" exposure as financial intermediaries.

Why? At the time, the "carry trade" was highly profitable because of the low regulatory risk weightings assigned to the higher tranches of these structured securities. This circumstance became the main source of the banking "crisis," which then led to forced mergers, nationalizations, and taxpayer bailouts—the impact of which continues today.

In effect, the banks buffered the shock to asset managers, which otherwise would have taken even greater losses than they actually booked. But asset managers were hardly immune. **Figure 2** shows one aspect of the crisis—stock prices—in the context of previous financial crises; in the case of the United States, the 2007–08 crisis brought the second-largest drop in stock prices at least since accurate records began to be kept in the 1870s and probably in all of US history.[4]

[4]The 13 market declines shown in Figure 2 are not the 13 largest over the nearly 300-year period shown; they were chosen for both severity and association with a particular economic event or crisis. Severe declines occurred also in 1917, 1937, 1940–1941, and other time periods.

Figure 2. **Historical Stock Market Losses in Financial Crises: United Kingdom and United States** (percentage from peak)

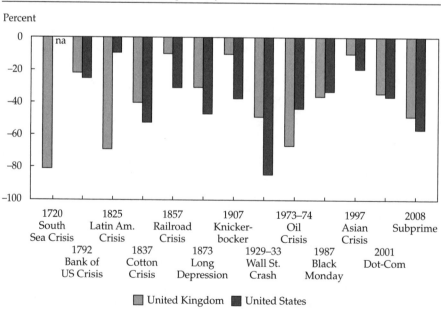

As it turned out, most asset classes experienced huge losses in 2007–2008, which impaired pension funds' ability to meet their DB obligations, caused DC savings balances to shrink dramatically, and eroded the overall size of assets in investment funds.

The crisis subsequently led to fewer, larger, and even more complex and interconnected financial intermediaries, and its aftermath has arguably increased rather than decreased the world's exposure to systemic risk. Living in this new world poses a whole set of postcrisis challenges for asset managers, both in serving their clients well and in devising new business models.

Not surprisingly, therefore, global finance continues to face a new regulatory environment, a change that has occurred in the aftermath of every significant financial shock in modern history. Taxpayers continue to show little patience with behavior they regard as posing new risks to the system and, even worse, as privatizing returns and socializing risk. The memory of taxpayer losses and risks borne at the height of the crisis remains surprisingly fresh and durable in people's minds today and underpins the political will to move beyond "business as usual" toward a more robust financial infrastructure.

Bolstering capital is the centerpiece of systemic-risk mitigation everywhere. Few reminders are needed of how undercapitalized major financial intermediaries were at the height of the crisis. In some cases, adequate capitalization of financial firms (notably, nonbank financial intermediaries) remains a work in progress. Beyond that issue, key initiatives focus on asset origination, assessing asset quality in light of the failure of rating agencies to identify "toxic" assets during the crisis, incentive-compatible approaches to compensation, carve-outs or "ring fencing" of activities that arguably do not belong in systemically sensitive financial intermediaries, and consumer protection in asset origination.

The task is to improve significantly the safety and soundness of financial intermediation while preserving as much as possible of the industry's efficiency, innovativeness, and competitiveness. As this effort proceeds, no part of the banking or shadow banking system,[5] including asset management, is spared the need to respond in a sensible and sustainable way.

From a *functional* perspective, these challenges focus on growth, risk management, and costs; from a *sector* perspective, they focus on pension funds, mutual funds, alternative investment funds, and private wealth. This approach forms a 3 × 4 matrix as an organizing framework for this study.

---

[5]Shadow banking refers to financial institutions that act like banks in that they transform maturities of financial claims but are not supervised like banks; sometimes, shadow banks are regulated institutions operating in the less transparent sectors of the market.

The immediate impact of the recent turbulence on the three industry attributes and four industry segments was to trigger dramatic declines in AUM as well as asset management industry revenues based on AUM and investment performance. A parallel impact affected clients. The financial shock clearly stressed existing business models. Asset management companies suffered much greater pressure on both risk management and cost control than they had previously experienced.

Many clients became much more risk conscious and cost sensitive in this environment, one in which already elusive asset management outperformance is even harder to locate and there are few places to hide from exposure to systemic risk. Convincing clients that cost control (and the technology supporting it) lies close to the heart of an asset manager's strategy—and that available risk management techniques are as advanced as possible—is surely as important today as it was before the financial turbulence. Both dimensions of asset management—risk management and cost control—lie at the core of any credible and durable strategy in this industry, including one that will translate into a favorable future-growth profile.

To be sure, global AUM in all sectors of the industry should continue to show impressive growth, but that growth will have a different geographical profile than before and will require serious progress on the risk management and cost management fronts.

Figure 3 and **Figure 4** show how personal income is related to managed assets, by country. Note that larger incomes and assets are inversely related to assets held in bank deposits. This aspect suggests ample room for industry growth as economic development progresses and diffuses in various parts of the world, a process that is well under way. **Table 2** provides a geographical breakdown of mutual fund and exchange-traded fund (ETF) assets in 2014; **Table 3** provides asset allocations in US mutual funds in 2014.[6]

The following sections provide discussions of the dynamics of the key asset management sectors: pension funds, mutual funds and related open-end asset pools, hedge funds and alternative asset pools, and private wealth management (both onshore and offshore).

---

[6]See also Oliver Wyman, *Personal Financial Assets Report 2013* (www.oliverwyman.com/content/dam/oliver-wyman/global/en/files/archive/2013/2013_Oliver_Wyman_PFA_report.pdf).

Figure 3. **Income Levels and Financial Deepening, 2013** (GDP per capita at year-end market exchange rates)

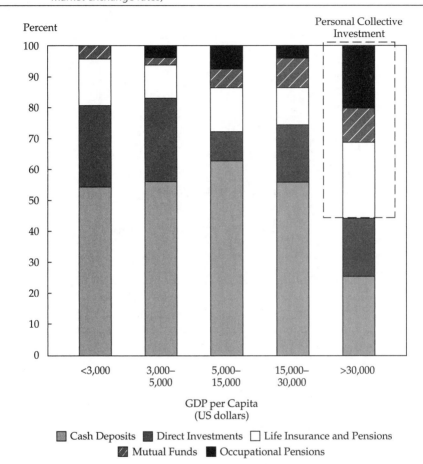

Source: Oliver Wyman, *Personal Financial Assets Report 2013* (www.oliverwyman.com/content/dam/oliver-wyman/global/en/files/archive/2013/2013_Oliver_Wyman_PFA_report.pdf).

Figure 4. **Share of Personal Financial Assets (PFA) Kept in Bank Accounts, Year-End 2013** (2013 data at market exchange rates)

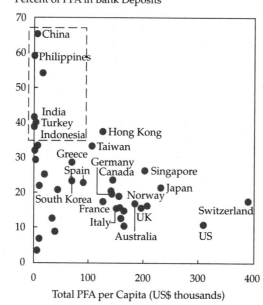

Source: Wyman, *Personal Financial Assets Report 2013.*

Table 2. Total Mutual Fund and ETF Assets, Year-End 2014

Global Area	Percentage
Worldwide[a]	
United States	53%
Europe	29
Africa and Asia Pacific	11
Other Americas	6
United States[b]	
Domestic equity funds	42
World equity funds	14
Bond funds	21
Money market funds	15
Hybrid and other funds[c]	8

[a]US$33.4 trillion.
[b]US$17.8 trillion.
[c]Includes ETFs—both registered and not registered under the Investment Company Act of 1940—that invest primarily in commodities, currencies, and futures.

Source: 2015 Investment Company Institute Fact Book.

Table 3. Asset Allocation in US Mutual Funds, 2014

Asset Class	Percentage
Equity	52%
Bond	22
Money market	17
Hybrid	9

Note: Total US mutual fund assets = US$15.9 trillion.

Source: 2015 Investment Company Institute Fact Book.

3. Pension Funds

The global population exceeded 7 billion by the end of 2012, and current demographic projections put the number at 9 billion by 2050—a much slower growth rate than in the recent past, but still growth. Tested many times over the years, the dire warnings of Thomas Malthus (1766–1834) have thus far proved inaccurate for a host of reasons, most of them having to do with productivity growth and technological advancement. But as mothers often warn their children, "Just you wait." Sooner or later, demographic pressure may exceed sustainability, although the pace will likely be closer to that of a boiling frog than a catastrophe.

Meanwhile, we have plenty of things to worry about. Global population growth masks dramatic geographical and structural changes that will put pressure on economic and social systems long before any demographic tipping point is reached.

Between now and 2050, the global population under age 25 is expected to hold steady at about 3 billion, but the population exceeding age 60 is projected to increase by 1.25 billion—the product of current high fertility and past declines in child mortality in key developing regions. Dependency rates—the ratio of retirees (age 65 and older) to those of working age (age 20–64)—in developing countries have been falling, but they will increase dramatically in the years ahead. These countries will begin to experience the rapid growth that is already happening in Europe, Japan, and the rest of the developed world, where the ratio will double by 2050. Only Southeast and South Asia, the Middle East, and Africa are likely to escape the dependency pressure cooker in the same time frame.

Overall demographics are further clouded by increased consumption by older people, which is largely driven by the increased cost of medical care, including long-term care. Higher incomes and such public policies as tax and social support systems have encouraged earlier retirement, and the result in many countries has been to increase both dependency and consumption. The impact has varied widely by country, however, and by how the resulting "life-cycle deficits" are financed—that is, public sector support, intergenerational transfers within families, or accumulated assets. Recent studies suggest that public transfers and personal assets finance most of these deficits and will continue to do so.

The most endangered retirement arrangements are national pension systems that rely heavily on public sector support and depend on current retirement contributions (so-called pay-as-you-go systems). Some of these plans incorporate essentially fictitious "trust funds" invested in government debt securities, but the trust funds have no economic impact. Many such systems were established under political conditions that encouraged generous promises to retirees and were built on optimistic economic growth assumptions.

Such systems now confront a stark reality: They can reduce benefits by increasing the retirement age, increasing taxes on pension benefits, or limiting benefit indexation to reduce the value of benefits in real terms. Alternatively, they can significantly raise pension contributions by current workers, a change that increases intergenerational transfers and runs into the reality of adverse demographics.

Least vulnerable are well-provisioned pension systems that combine a baseline public benefit program with dedicated, prefunded pools of financial assets provided by employers, individuals, or both. Employers may provide DB pension plans, which obligate them to maintain asset levels actuarially sufficient to meet their obligations—usually backed by guarantees to manage the risk that the asset pools will turn out to be underfunded. In cases of underfunded DB pension plans, employers are usually obliged to top up the funding unless the shortfall is restructured in bankruptcy.

Alternatively, employers can sponsor DC plans for their employees, with various investment options. Many employers have replaced DB plans with DC plans to shift the pension funding risk to employees while offering a broad range of investment choices to plan participants.

In addition to public baseline plans (e.g., Social Security in the United States) and employer-sponsored plans, well-structured pension systems include individual savings programs encouraged by favorable tax treatment for contributions and/or withdrawals. Set at realistic levels under conservative assumptions about demographics, life expectancy, economic growth, and financial returns—and permitting broad portfolio diversification options—such "three-tier" systems are likely to be the most capable of meeting their commitments and the least vulnerable to future economic and financial shocks.

Given these realities, the variation among countries in the design of their pension systems is impressively large. Among developed countries, plans extend from rock-solid systems, like those of the Nordic countries and Switzerland, to disaster-prone systems, like those of Spain and Greece. Even such rich countries as France and Germany are looking at major funding gaps down the road.

Among some formerly developing countries—many of which benefit from much better demographics than the developed countries, at least in the medium term—existing systems vary widely. Singapore and Chile have pension systems that are both universal (mandatory) and well funded, whereas in Argentina, private pensions have been seized by the government (with participants rolled into the pay-as-you-go national plan). In much of Africa and parts of Asia, pension systems do not exist. Fortunately, the slower aging of the population in many of these countries gives them time to design properly funded and managed pension schemes.

In the end, the amalgam of national pension systems and the great desirability of properly funding them to avoid serious economic and political repercussions create a bright picture for the future growth of suppliers of pension services. Expansion of viable prefunded public and private pension systems is by far the lowest-cost alternative for countries confronting their demographic realities. And these providers stand to reap big dividends as disproportionate growth in pension pools spurs the development of broader and deeper capital markets that are likely to produce additional growth dividends.

Key issues confronting the global pension fund industry are risks, costs, and growth. Major risks range from demographic change and increased regulation to stiff competition and adequacy of investment returns. Costs and efficiency have become critical, both in supporting adequate pension benefits and in distinguishing among competitors in an industry where a durable performance advantage is not easy to achieve. Such an advantage depends heavily on coherence in investment processes, economies of scale and outsourcing, onsite transactions and asset management infrastructure, and application of state-of-the-art information technology.

Clearly, the key challenge facing pension funds today is the rapidly aging population, which will force fund trustees to provide participants with payouts over a longer period of time. Therefore, pension funds and insurance companies that offer retirement products need to earn returns as high as markets will allow while generating stable cash flows for the retiring population, a situation that puts great demands on them. So, in the next 10–20 years, the entire industry would be well advised to restructure to manage risk, provide stable cash flows, and tailor solutions to the specific needs of corporate and public sector sponsors and individual participants.

One of the factors that could lead the industry to a successful future is consolidation. The simultaneous requirements of higher performance after costs, lower risk, and more stable cash flows may be met more easily in big financial groups that can invest in many different asset classes and provide a stable and reliable risk management system. In this chapter, I examine the contours of risk, cost, and growth that will play a determining role in the pension fund component of the global asset management industry.

Growth Challenges Facing the Pension Fund Industry

As previously noted, the global pension fund industry faces a bright future as a provider of prefunded pension cash flows. This prospect affects products ranging from annuities sold by insurers to DC assets lodged in mutual funds. AUM are likely to grow substantially faster than the real economy. The sources of that growth and some of the challenges it creates are discussed under these headings: changing demographics, benefits and competition, internationalization, and regulation.

Changing Demographics. Increased private retirement savings resulting from changing demographics will represent a major source of growth and opportunity for pension and insurance-related retirement funds. The need to save more and retire later will spur growth in the industry. With the trend shifting from DB schemes to DC schemes, this change represents both a major source of growth and a disruptive structural shift.

The DB-to-DC shift comes with a significant risk for incumbent managers of DB plan assets. It opens up space for other types of managers and such competing products as actively managed mutual funds and index funds.

Other factors to be considered, particularly in Europe and the United States, are the need for young people to start saving earlier and higher mandatory retirement ages because of people living longer. Together with filling the gap caused by underfunding in the baseline public DB schemes, this trend creates the framework for a larger market and increases the scope for expansion. For firms providing pension services, this expansion requires

1. a proper definition of the market that is best suited to the particular organization;

2. a clear setting of the strategic direction, a sensible operational structure, and cultural adaptability (i.e., national, regional, or global);

3. the use of existing distribution channels or the establishment of new ones (third party or otherwise) that are specifically geared to the pension sector by offering attractive, off-the-shelf, and cost-effective products;

4. the adoption of a corporate policy of systematic implementation and execution based on clear performance criteria; and

5. greater flexibility in the choice of funds offered to pension schemes and insurance policies, particularly in Europe, where the current situation is rigid.

The goal is to take the "value chain," break it into its components, and figure out the global dimensions of each component. In one component (e.g., a state or local pension plan in the United States), the global dimension might be close to zero; in another component—say, an insurance company with global reach—it might be extremely important. This kind of segmentation should help ensure that funds are specifically tailored to meet investors' varying retirement needs.

Benefits and Competition. If the bulk of the pension fund management industry is moving from DB to DC plans, perhaps the best way for the prospective beneficiary to evaluate how good a provider is—given that in DC plans, the risk is taken by investors themselves—is to use a predetermined measure of performance. An example would be to assess DB plan performance in terms of return relative to the liability and DC plan performance in terms of absolute return.

Expansion of the DC pension model provides the market opportunity to offer DC pension schemes and supportive services. In Europe, national (fixed-benefit) pension schemes are being reduced—as has been discussed for Social Security in the United States—and people are being encouraged to make additional pension savings. So, the traditional pension fund is being transformed into an ordinary investment fund, with collective risk sharing reduced or eliminated. These retirement schemes can be individual pension contracts or collective pension schemes through an employer or trade union and are typically in addition to the bare-minimum public scheme.

Many countries are experiencing a greatly increased role for private DC plans in filling the gap as state and employer-based retirement provision declines. But exactly how this growth will occur is not clear. One of the challenges will be to work out how best to market a pension plan to ordinary savers—as a savings plan with a well-defined current market value or as an annuity-type promise or expected pension flow starting at a given retirement age?

On the asset side, there is scope for widening the set of assets held by pension plans. Many risks can be traded in financial markets; innovations include longevity bonds, which pay off according to a cohort's mortality rates, and social bonds, which pay off according to the success of some remedial program. All these new products and services (with their emphasis on saving more and retiring later) will spur competition in the marketplace. With the industry evidently thinking in terms of delivering a *process* rather than a *product*, this competition represents a growth opportunity.

Meanwhile, competition is likely to increase across the entire spectrum of products and services related to DC pensions. The effect may be to accelerate the erosion of DB pensions and open up the possibility of expanding market share in that segment, but competition may also cost the more traditional pension fund providers market share. The industry must decide whether it wants to base itself on absolute or relative performance, although in practice, that decision will probably be made on a case-by-case basis. The industry will have to identify and generate the product mix that clients want in each pension market segment, whether DB or DC. Product time to market will play a significant role. Product innovation will also be a key factor in promoting industry growth; the use of mutual funds by the larger players as a vehicle for pension and retirement savings plans may increase.

Internationalization. Globalization of the pension business will involve both an international client base of pension plan sponsors and international investments held in the portfolios. With few practical restrictions on capital flows, managers can pursue pension portfolio asset allocation on a worldwide scale.

As noted earlier, pension systems in some countries (e.g., France, Italy, Spain, and Portugal) are massively underfunded, making them potentially fast-growing markets for pension fund product offerings. As a source of new customers for new products, emerging markets similarly represent potential growth opportunities for the industry. China, India, and other rapidly developing countries are gaining wealth, which boosts private consumption. Latin America—with Brazil, Chile, and Mexico in the lead—is already building up a major pension fund management industry.

A key question is whether these markets will be sufficiently mature for US, European, and other developed-country players to enter yet offer enough future growth prospects to make entering worthwhile. The markets themselves are heterogeneous. Competition between European and US-based investment managers, pension funds, and insurance funds, on the one hand, and similar funds domiciled in Asia, the Middle East, and Latin America, on the other hand, is likely to increase as developing-country governments seek to promote the establishment of local industries. So, the challenges will be market penetration and whether to grow organically or acquire a local distribution channel or pension fund player.

As the share of emerging economies in global economic output rises, these markets will become an essential source of demand for investment products and management. This trend will logically spur a global relocation of portfolios, although tax differences make many pension markets difficult to penetrate. But with the introduction of International Financial Reporting Standards (IFRS) and, at least in Europe, gradual harmonization of economic policies, entering markets and sustaining market access should become less difficult in the coming years.

Among the industry's leaders will be those pension and insurance fund managers that acquire and accumulate the necessary know-how to exploit the growth opportunities offered by internationalization, including expansion to emerging markets. A critical factor is the ability of a manager to apply a global approach, combined with local skills and expertise, to extend its pension and insurance fund franchise into targeted markets abroad. By doing so, a manager may be able to create a global investment management and distribution platform and interface with local outlets to accommodate local market tastes, customs, and traditions.

Regulation. Although the pension and insurance fund management business is likely to continue to internationalize, it will face regulatory challenges on a country-by-country basis. Regulation has three dimensions, a combination of micro and macro factors: the regulatory overlay itself, asset selection, and market entry. With intensified regulatory activity and rules on the horizon, investment management companies will have to develop strategies and products that comply in a wide variety of jurisdictions.

The changes resulting from the regulatory imperative generally take place at the strategic level. They are no longer at the business unit level or at the product level, as was sometimes true in the past. Such a strategic positioning must take into account various initiatives, including the Dodd–Frank Act (Wall Street Reform and Consumer Protection Act of 2010) in the United States, MiFID in Europe, AIFMD, EMIR, Solvency II, UCITS IV, and others.[7]

Thus, a comprehensive, custom-built, and sophisticated regulatory compliance program seems mandatory for success. Separating the winners from the losers in an era of increased pension fund regulation will be the ability to (1) diagnose the prevailing regulatory trends correctly, (2) anticipate the changes that are coming, and (3) implement the necessary measures to accommodate them. On the one hand, increased regulation may help spur product standardization, which will lead to more standardized and understandable pension and insurance fund products. On the other hand, increased regulation could promote higher levels of concentration in the pension fund

---

[7]MiFID refers to the Markets in Financial Instruments Directive; AIFMD refers to the Alternative Investment Fund Managers Directive; EMIR stands for European Market Infrastructure Regulation; and UCITS stands for the Undertakings for Collective Investment in Transferable Securities directive.

industry, encouraging players to operate across markets, which, in turn, may affect the competitive dynamics of the industry.

Although these drivers may be good for the industry as a whole, they probably make it tougher for small players to enter the market and succeed. Size and scale are good for asset management organizations that have the necessary resources and integrated operational platforms. Cross-border firms may well be better equipped than their locally based counterparts to deal with regional and global regulation.

Risk Challenges

The four key risks in the pension and insurance sector for both the short term and the medium term involve demographics, competition, regulatory risk, and investment risk.

Back to Demographics. The aging population represents a potential risk. As discussed previously, nearly 30% of the population in the Western world will be over 60 by 2025. The aging of the population will require effective retirement plans and higher savings rates than presently exist. At the same time, life expectancy is on the increase worldwide. From 1980 to 2010, the actual (as opposed to statutory) retirement age—at least in Europe—declined, although it is expected to increase as national governments raise the mandatory retirement age to ease the strain on depleted budgets.

In this environment, pension savings have failed to grow at the same rate as the number of years of retirement that the savings are intended to pay for. As the population ages, pension coverage must be extended. This need has put pressure on both national and private pension schemes. Attempts to restore some balance between pension costs and benefits have proved politically controversial.

In terms of DB agreements, given the low yields obtainable under current market conditions, funding deficits have already arisen—in, for example, many US public and corporate plans and in France and Germany. Moreover, there is a very real risk of the deficits affecting payouts to beneficiaries.

In some jurisdictions, a large number of pension schemes have a DC character at their core but are accompanied by a guaranteed minimum yield or minimum payment. These pension schemes also have a potential funding problem in current market conditions. When reserves are tight and a funding problem looms, the regulator will typically insist on safe, conservative investments, which limit the return that pension savers can expect to see.

The pension fund industry needs to recognize that the growth of private collective and independent pension schemes represents a continued broad-based favorable trend with a high degree of sustainability. Several responses seem required:

- Adoption of measures that provide highly specialized solutions to accommodate the aging population trend in the pension area, turning it into a source of competitive advantage. Assuming that the expected change in retirement lengths or dependency ratios is dictated by a combination of demographic patterns and governments, innovative solutions imply dealing with uncertain retirement ages and uncertain life expectancies. The former are related to the flexibility offered to pensioners regarding when to take their pensions and the rewards for delaying, and the latter are related to the ability to hedge longevity risk or spread it in various ways among pension scheme members.

- The need for the industry to proactively and professionally manage the increasing complexity of the pension marketplace. Meeting this need involves improved risk and liquidity management, effective portfolio allocation, and increased effort to educate customers about the fact that pension and insurance products are more complex than banking products and require a higher degree of risk taking to deliver the required performance.

- Development of a proper process for benchmarking performance, which must be done with a coordinated effort at the industry level. Such a process would not only provide transparency to investors but also be instrumental in appropriately implementing information technology (IT) applications and processes.

Increased Competition. Most reformed pension systems today seem to combine elements of the public baseline, employer-supported, and individual components noted earlier. Each element serves a function, and they work well together. Therefore, single-component pension schemes may not be the best at achieving the overall policy goals of a pension system. Different components are exposed to different risks, and the correlation between those risks is far less than perfect.

A key policy issue for governments designing pension and social insurance systems is to balance redistributive, savings, and insurance functions. Each pension component serves these three functions in different ways. Depending on a country's situation, combining the approaches into a three-component pension system may be the most effective way to balance pension objectives.

The case for multicomponent pension schemes raises the prospect of increased competition from new providers, which represents a major source of risk for the established providers of pension schemes. This competition would benefit customers if it provided a level playing field among funds and countries. The lack of such a level playing field is a real danger, however, because regulation can skew and distort the market in favor of some and against others. The effect can worsen as sharper competition emerges—for example, when tax incentives are compromised and pension guarantees disappear.

Competition will enlarge the role of operational platforms, where the management of information takes place together with the execution of decisions. A pension plan could, for example, gain a competitive advantage because it has the right operational platform and can defray its costs by being affiliated with a major financial conglomerate, whether in the insurance, pension, or bank sector. This possibility suggests that future high-performance pension managers will be companies that are quick to develop and provide expert asset management advisory and consultancy services attuned to pension requirements. Possible responses to competition risk include the following:

1. *Achieving a size that takes advantage of economies of scale.* This response would create a sort of entry barrier to ward off competition from new market entrants.

2. *Introducing value management mechanisms to monitor each link in the investment management chain.* For this purpose, the implementation of business- and IT-related measures would increase the competitiveness of front- and back-office functions, distribution, asset management, and private wealth and advisory services to secure and enhance transparency.

3. *Adopting straight-through processing (STP)* and other automated functions to ensure that products, data, and valuations remain synchronized among all the parties in the value chain.

4. *Coordinating with other products offered by the same financial conglomerate.* Here, the focus is on examining and deciding whether, for example, more mutual fund products should be added to the pension and insurance fund product line to enhance competitiveness.

Regulatory Risk. The introduction of new regulations and the increased pace of regulatory reform pose risks for the pension fund management industry in that these changes create uncertainty and require a risk-related response from the industry. For the investment management industry as a whole, the regulatory and compliance challenges in the years ahead will be unprecedented.

Among the changes to be considered at the strategic, tactical, systemic, and operational levels are the new regulatory frameworks and demands of, for example, the Dodd–Frank Act in the United States, UCITS IV in the

European Union (EU), and, internationally, the new tax rules and standards primarily embodied in IFRS 9, Financial Instruments, in reference to financial instruments.

Regulation is both good and bad. It endows the industry with a great deal of credibility but also creates regulatory uncertainty and increases complexity. Among the industry winners in this sphere will be those companies that recognize early the importance of having an optimal operational platform (including the right investment management system) and functionality to deal with the challenge of increased regulation. Many responses to this challenge can be envisioned:

1. *Introducing internal compliance procedures and mechanisms to deal with the burden of increased regulation.* In this context, the choice of the right operational platform—one that is sufficiently agile and flexible to take into account all the existing and forthcoming regulatory changes and apply them to the business process—may be the key operational response to the regulatory challenge.

2. *Exerting influence on management to clarify or dispel uncertainty surrounding new regulations (e.g., UCITS IV and AIFMD).* Examples would be by reviewing marketing materials and making them clearer, harmonizing tax requirements—especially internationally, across major geographical areas (e.g., the EU)—and reducing the administrative burden. This response also involves the design and construction of operational and IT structures and platforms that are flexible and attuned to change in the event of new regulations and standards.

3. *Involving the regulators*—that is, lobbying to ensure that regulatory decision making and the implementation of new standards reflect the knowledge and experience of industry participants. Overall, there is a sense that transparency is not always necessarily a good thing. The pension fund industry has a great deal of work to do with the regulators in settling on the optimal amount of regulation and transparency as well as the type of transparency required—that is, information that is regulation driven, reputation driven, industry driven, or a combination of all three.

Investment Risk. Investment risk in pension fund management covers a broad area, including the market and business risks related to meeting pension fund and insurance company liabilities. At least three types of risk affect the industry: (1) market risk in terms of volatility and other aspects of asset performance, (2) "fat-tail" risk, and (3) long-term risk, sometimes portrayed as the risk of having overpaid for an asset. Although market trends in products and prices may be difficult to forecast accurately in terms of direction, magnitude, and timing, their associated risks can be identified with some success. A successful risk management model must be able to address dynamic risk budgeting in a fast-changing and volatile world to ensure the adequacy of pension fund balances.

Diversification is only one way of reducing risk. "Tail events" (extreme events represented by the tail of a bell curve) are fatter and occur more often than almost all models predict. Moreover, not all value-at-risk (VaR) models measure investment risk adequately, so they may not have the desired effect of helping managers control this risk. In the hazardous hunt for alpha when the basic, safe return is low, pension institutions and the individual pension savers have an inducement to take greater risks. It seems logical that the winners in the pension and insurance fund industry will be companies that can accurately assess the risks of their assets and their pension liabilities.

In this context, pension and insurance fund organizations need to recognize that new market trends (e.g., absolute versus relative returns) are all part of the process of a marketplace in constant flux. So, asset management must be effectively and efficiently aligned with IT and process strategies. The industry must be able to identify the most harmful risks and diversify to reduce the overall risk embedded in pension fund management.

Risk management includes examining how well the pension fund industry is faring in terms of risk and return, assessment of tail risk, and implementation of suitable VaR models supported by integrated IT platforms. It also suggests the adoption of appropriate investment strategies to guard against market, credit, and liquidity risk (options, hedging, short and long positions, etc.). These investment strategies should be part of an overall approach that considers both the asset side and the liability side and offers pension schemes tailored to the assets and liabilities of the particular sector or company.

Is the performance measurement horizon for pension investments long enough to allow pension funds to reap the benefits of a long-term strategy? If so, does that horizon imply that pension funds enjoy lower investment risk (e.g., reduced sensitivity to liquidity and fire-sale risks)? Designing appropriate risk management strategies for institutions with long investment horizons is critical for the industry.

If strategies are inappropriate, sharp deteriorations in the investment climate may force institutions to liquidate or otherwise reposition their portfolios just when the costs of repositioning are highest. The industry should be able to identify which types of risk become diversifiable in the longer time frame that would not be diversifiable for short-term traditional asset managers. Whether this area is a source of competitive advantage remains unclear.

Finally, it is important to increase industry-driven transparency of operating procedures to help identify best practices. In the process, regulatory compliance will be supported by IT solutions. The industry must develop measures and exercises to benchmark best practices, clearly defining the parameters of and barriers to competition.

Cost Challenges

Costs are important in the pension sector—as in all areas of asset management—because of the certainty with which they affect pension benefits in an environment of uncertain returns. Important cost issues are technology and infrastructure, investment processes, general outsourcing, and economies of scale.

Technology and Infrastructure. This topic combines a number of cost-related factors: technology management and infrastructure costs, manual processing costs, and processes to manage change and flexibility.

To control costs effectively, the pension fund organization's platform must be managed well. In the area of technology management, far more difficult and complex products and services will need to be handled in the future than in the past. For example, investment in illiquid assets requires more data and is more costly than investment in traditional liquid investments. Moreover, the increased use of derivatives increases the costs of clearing and margining. All of these factors call for a flexible platform to ensure effective management of the operation.

Infrastructure costs have increased, including those associated with the implementation of internal cost controls and the introduction of customized operational practices tailored to the asset management business (e.g., reduction of settlement risk). Manual processing is still common in the pension and insurance fund sector. It ranges from handling corporate actions to various reconciliation processes to communication with the end client.

To cope with these challenges, pension fund organizations must have an adaptable and flexible platform that provides corporate decision makers with the real-time information they need in the most cost-effective way. Cost-effectiveness requires a calculated selection, choice, and implementation of an operational platform strategy and a secure alignment of the platform with business and IT mandates over a long time horizon, including automated workflows, STP, and effective client communication services.

This approach hardly means a reduction in human interface and human resource investment. Pension fund asset management is becoming increasingly complex, and manual processes often cannot be easily downsized or streamlined. Indeed, the growing importance of less liquid asset classes increases the need for direct manual management.

The pension fund cost challenge is to try to standardize processes as much as possible while accepting the need for long-term development of human resources. This effort requires efficient cost management. Some 85% of a pension fund management firm's budget is tied up in the cost of human capital; only 15% goes to the rest—IT platforms, technology, and other costs.

Finally, because the regulatory environment and the marketplace itself are in constant flux, flexible processes need to be in place to ensure effective operational cost management.

Investment Processes. New international regulations and rules pose cost challenges. For example, the EU insurance industry's Solvency II directive brings a fundamental change to the regulation of insurance companies in the EU.[8] In both the short and the medium term, the data management and data quality requirements resulting from Solvency II will pose a major cost challenge for insurance companies and their asset management businesses.

Because higher risk requires higher solvency capital, insurance companies will generally aim for low investment risk. This change will alter their asset allocation strategies and have an impact on the industry as a whole. The complexity of asset management for insurance companies is high because of the differences in the individual investment portfolios of insurance companies and differences in granularity among the various requirements. Thus, the companies require accurate and immediate quoted market prices and yields of bonds and equities, detailed information on derivatives, geographical data on the individual assets, and information on guarantees.

In addition to Solvency II, asset managers in the EU insurance fund sector face legal and regulatory requirements that will increase the importance of an early response to the changes. An efficient, timely, and structured approach can reduce costs and save resources. Leaders in the pension and insurance fund sector will have to be quick to recognize these factors—implementing the right investment processes and reducing the time to market of new pension products and insurance schemes.

The main response to this challenge is to define an investment strategy/policy that analyzes securities, minimizes portfolio risk, evaluates performance, and revises the portfolio in as cost-effective and automated a way as possible without jeopardizing the integrity of the investment process. This approach involves (1) identification and application of reliable and transparent

---

[8]For a description of the regulation, see, for example, "What Is Solvency II?" at www.lloyds.com/the-market/operating-at-lloyds/solvency-ii/about/what-is-solvency-ii.

investment processes; (2) adoption of a cost-efficient operational platform; (3) introduction of an effective way to measure, monitor, and manage the liquidity risk in investment processes; and (4) establishment of viable risk–return profiles and benchmarks to determine allocation in the investment process. Ensuring that performance measurement plays a pivotal role in the investment process and supporting and strengthening the risk management system with IT-integrated solutions are key factors in this effort.

To be successful, pension and insurance fund managers will have to recognize that risk management constitutes an integral part of the overall investment process. The ability to assess the need to provide transparency and to ensure the integrity and consistency of the data and models used in the investment process ranks at the top of the list of any risk management strategy.

Outsourcing. Many pension and insurance fund managers apparently continue to use in-house asset management for domestic and other relatively familiar asset classes and use external asset managers for more specialized investments. This practice raises challenges as well as opportunities in terms of costs. Outsourced functions often include fund distribution, back-office operations, IT, and portfolio management.

Outsourcing affects direct costs, the quality of service obtained, and the cost of monitoring quality. Outsourcing solutions must be able to integrate state-of-the-art technology with business-specific knowledge to bring about top-notch performance and uninterrupted operations. This approach will yield reliable and flexible management tools and operational workflow systems that focus on quality processing. This goal is often achieved by developing in-house systems, based on an open architecture, as part of a continuous, sustainable investment process to support market and distribution demands.

Pension and insurance fund managers should identify the areas to be outsourced and find the right suppliers. This effort involves identifying areas where the managers themselves do not have a competitive advantage and then defining the process for screening and selecting external suppliers.

Outsourcing is inevitably a front-office and due diligence function. Building systems to monitor and measure the quality of the outsourced product or service, determining ways to measure the effectiveness of outsourcing, and identifying the areas where it would best be applied are critical factors in the pension fund management industry. Outsourcing should be assessed in terms not only of cost savings but also of the impact on quality, flexibility, control, and customization to address varying pension needs.

Scale and Consolidation. The pension and insurance fund sector is experiencing increasing concentration because of the marketing muscle of the largest players and rising market-entry costs. When mergers and acquisitions are used as a technique to spur consolidation and concentration, stand-alone pension institutions are typically not organized as commercial companies and thus cannot be acquired, raising the question of what is the "optimal" level of competition as well as a number of cost-related issues.

A key cost challenge is to identify and exploit cheap distribution channels for pension savings products. Market competition has only limited ability to drive down costs because costs tend to be opaque and pension beneficiaries tend to do poorly at comparing products. Existing low-cost distribution channels (e.g., company-sponsored DB pension schemes) are increasingly under threat. Employers have little interest in providing pensions and are inhibited in doing so by the need to recognize pension liabilities in accounting statements and by the fear of potential legal liability if things go wrong. Even company-sponsored DC pension programs entail costs that firms sometimes strive to avoid.

Consequently, the pension fund industry already appears to be moving toward a relatively larger scale in terms of centralized technology and optimal work processes. It remains limited, however, in its ability to grow and to reap the benefits of economies of scale. Technical and fiscal barriers to market entry continue to impede consolidation across borders, particularly in the EU, and these obstacles must be overcome to reduce acquisition costs. There are several answers to this challenge.

First, pension and insurance companies that manage pension assets should set a clear course of action, with the "end game" firmly in mind as a source of strength and cost synergies playing a secondary yet important role. To do so, they must adopt processes and systems that scale up well in order to take on more volume, better apportion costs, and fully utilize capacity.

Second, there are two main paths to improved capacity utilization: consolidation and cooperation. Consolidation can lead to a "conglomerate discount" and (possibly) to a "geographical premium" when pursued across national pension fund markets. Many organizations are reluctant to consolidate, however, unless they are the dominant party; cooperation (e.g., by setting up joint ventures or alliances) may be more appealing.

The cost of market entry in the pension fund sector is likely to rise, creating problems for small players and new entrants. At the same time, this trend will increase the prospect of monopolistic behavior and a concomitant rise in pension-related fees as competitors are squeezed out of an increasingly competitive and cost-driven market. This outcome poses the question of whether scale should take the form of a complete "wrap" package offered to pension funds or, alternatively, multiple packages tailored to meet diverse retirement needs.

Summary

Challenges associated with risk, cost, and growth are interrelated and affect pension funds and pension-related insurance funds to varying degrees. Changing demographics will alter pension-funding patterns, creating cost challenges but growth opportunities for pension funds, insurance reserves, and those who manage these asset pools.

Greater market volatility, increased financial instability, and material regulatory changes will affect business risk, cost, and growth. The resulting challenges and opportunities are not always equally important. The main drivers of success will be flexibility in strategic targeting and implementation, together with the adaptability of operations.

Scale, internationalization, and the right choice of operational platform are key determinants in promoting growth, mitigating risk, and controlling costs. Functional breadth in terms of retirement products is important, but large size (AUM) is also advantageous. Not only the investment side but also the transaction side and the information platform need to be well managed in terms of client services, risk management, and cost efficiency.

Indeed, the abilities of the operational platform form a common thread running through all the themes related to pension fund asset management. This platform is critical in promoting flexibility and in creating barriers to entry and exit that are central in determining the organization of the industry.

4. Mutual Funds

Compounding the traditional challenge of producing significant and durable excess returns, mutual funds emerged from the financial turbulence of 2007–2008 with their reputations among clients severely stressed. Almost all had failed to protect their investors from the broad market decline and increased volatility of the crisis. This outcome was perceived by many investors as a disaster, despite the stated intentions of many of the funds to move with the overall market, including in periods of decline.

Some funds incorporated structured financial products that they themselves failed to understand—and could not explain adequately to clients. Several major funds prevented their customers from redeeming their shares to avoid having to sell the underlying securities in disorderly markets. Others were lacking in the key areas of due diligence and risk management. The asset management industry as a whole was found deficient in transparency, effective risk control, and operating efficiency.

Consequently, the postcrisis era began with the industry facing skeptical, sharp-eyed, and cost-conscious investors who had not forgotten their recent experience, low-cost asset management alternatives, and regulatory changes.

The initial challenge to the mutual fund industry, therefore, is to (1) rebuild confidence in mutual funds and other collective investment vehicles while (2) dealing with intensified competition from several quarters and (3) formulating a constructive set of responses to the inevitable increase in regulatory pressure—some of which remains uncertain. The emphasis is on improved transparency at all levels—products, processes, costs, and compliance—and a fundamental reconsideration by top management of these issues as sources of competitive advantage.

Asset managers able to meet the challenges—in the face of competition from passive funds, hedge funds, and a number of nontraditional competitors—are likely to be most prominent among the winners in today's world, where business as usual is unlikely to produce the kind of growth, risk profile, or operating efficiency the industry has enjoyed in the past.

Sector Overview

Mutual funds pool the financial assets of retail (household) investors and purchase a portfolio of assets. The underlying assets typically share a common characteristic, such as stocks believed by the manager to be undervalued, large- or small-cap stocks, or fixed-income instruments representing domestic or foreign issuers. Investors enter a mutual fund by purchasing shares (typically from the fund management company itself rather than from another shareholder), and the net asset value (NAV) of each share is determined by dividing the net value of the portfolio by the number of outstanding shares. The mutual fund industry has enjoyed rapid growth over the past several decades, although there are wide differences among national financial markets in the development of the industry, in the composition of AUM, and in the "chemistry" of mutual fund marketing and distribution.

At year-end 2014, the NAV of mutual funds worldwide was roughly US$33.4 trillion (see Table 2 in Chapter 2).

In the United States, about 70% of households own mutual funds, principally for retirement. As discussed in Chapter 3, private DC retirement assets are expected to grow rapidly throughout the world, particularly in Europe. Mutual funds are a natural product for the retirement industry. They can be crafted into a platform that will actually help people plan effectively for retirement, which represents an opportunity for the development of suitable products and systems.

In the United States, home to about half of global mutual fund assets, mutual funds have traditionally been invested mainly in equities. In times of financial turmoil, however, investments shift from equity funds to money market funds. In 1975, more than 82% of fund AUM was allocated to equities, with a mere 10% and 8% to, respectively, bonds and money market instruments. By 1985, this picture had changed completely. Because of poor stock market performance in the 1970s and early 1980s and the substitution of money market mutual funds for bank savings products by households searching for higher yields, the equity component had declined to 24%, and money market funds were capturing 49%. By 2001, the US pattern of mutual fund investments had shifted yet again, with equities accounting for 57% of the total; money market funds, 25%; and bond funds, 18%.

During the financial turmoil of 2007–2008, mutual fund investments once again experienced a general flight to quality. The share of equity funds fell to 40%, while investments in money market funds rose to 40% of all mutual funds. The year 2008 was also the first year in which the mutual fund industry as a whole experienced a net cash outflow. Six years after the crisis, at the end of 2014, these numbers were equities, 52%; bonds, 22%; money market funds, 17%; and hybrid funds, 9% (refer to Table 3 in Chapter 2).

Mutual Fund Distribution

Countries differ widely in how mutual funds are distributed, which is linked to comparative mutual fund growth and structure. Mutual fund distribution through bank branches has dominated in such countries as Germany, France, and Spain; Italian distribution is roughly split between bank branches and independent sales forces. In the United Kingdom, distribution is concentrated among independent advisers, but financial supermarkets—where discount brokers offer a wide variety of funds—are increasingly popular. Cross-border trades in Europe are almost always handled in either Luxembourg or Ireland, which together account for more than 90% of the business.

The dominance of universal banks, savings banks, and cooperative banks as financial intermediaries in most continental European countries explains the high concentration of mutual fund distribution via branch networks. In the United States, large independent mutual fund firms compete with investment banks, insurance companies, discount brokers, and commercial banks. So, mutual funds are distributed in a much more heterogeneous structure. Moreover, in the United States, mutual funds are also distributed through employer-sponsored DC plans, which offer employees a variety of fund choices.

Table 4 shows the relative shares of distribution providers in the United States as of 2015. In the United States, full-service broker/dealers maintain large retail sales forces capable of penetrating the household sector. In recent years, discount brokers have made substantial inroads into mutual fund distribution. They compensate for reduced sales effort and limited investment advice with lower fees and expenses. Insurance agents account for a substantial share of US mutual fund distribution. They focus on mutual funds with an insurance wrapper, such as fixed and variable annuities and guaranteed investment contracts. Bank branches have traditionally played a limited role in the United States—a legacy of regulatory constraints. Thus, they account for a relatively small distribution share.

Table 4. Distribution Structure of the US Mutual Fund Industry, 2015

Distributor	Percentage
Independent fund advisers	80%
Non-US fund advisers	8
Insurance companies	5
Banks or thrifts	5
Brokerage firms	2

Note: The term "adviser" denotes mutual fund distributor.

Source: 2015 Investment Company Institute Fact Book.

Mutual fund distribution has undergone dramatic change. Distribution without advice is clearly most efficient over the internet, which means that transaction services can be separated from investment advice, both functionally and in terms of pricing. Robo-advisers offering advice over the internet have begun to have an impact. Still, advice can be delivered in disembodied form only in part. Any added value depends partly on interpretive information on investments and partly on personal counseling that the client must be willing to pay for. With this advice increasingly likely to come from independent financial planners in many markets, traditional distributors of mutual funds are finding encroachment from both sides and have had to react to maintain market share.

Regulatory change has also altered the role of "advice" in mutual fund distribution. In the United States, Registered Investment Advisers (RIAs) are obligated to follow a prescribed "know your customer" process and then apply a fiduciary standard of recommending the best available investment products to that customer. Brokers have been considered "salespeople," however, and are required only to follow a "suitability" standard in recommending investments.

RIAs typically are compensated directly by their clients or by their firms on the basis of AUM, whereas broker compensation is based largely on sales commissions. The blurred distinction in the eyes of clients took on increased importance during the financial crisis of 2007–2008 and, more generally, with brokers advising about retirement investments. Against heavy opposition from the brokerage industry, the US Securities and Exchange Commission (SEC) in 2015 reclassified the role of stockbrokers from selling "suitable" products to the higher investment advisory standard of acting as financial fiduciaries for clients, thus moving toward a converging of the classic "investment sales" and "investment advisory" roles. Whether this change will alleviate conflicts of interest that characterize mutual fund distribution remains to be seen.

Mutual Fund Competition

Competition among mutual funds can be the most intense in the entire financial system. This competition is heightened by analytical services that measure fund performance in terms of risk and return relative to indexes over different holding periods and assign ratings on the basis of fund performance. The fund-rating services are important because the vast majority of new investments flow into highly rated funds. These highly rated funds capture roughly three-quarters of all mutual fund assets. In addition, widely read business publications regularly release "scoreboards" of publicly available mutual funds based on such ratings and—together with specialized investment publications and information disseminated over the internet—have made mutual funds one of the most transparent parts of the retail financial services sector.

Despite clear warnings that past performance is no assurance of future results, a rise in the performance rankings often brings in a flood of new investments and management company revenues. Individual asset managers are compensated commensurately and sometimes move on to manage larger and more prestigious funds. Conversely, serious performance slippage causes investors to withdraw funds. And they take with them a good part of the manager's bonus and perhaps, given that the firm's revenues are vitally dependent on new investments and total AUM, even take the manager's job.

A gradual decline has occurred in the sophistication of the average investor in many markets. Mutual funds have become more retail oriented, mass market, and interlinked with pension schemes. Therefore, performance ratings, name recognition, and "branding" have become increasingly important in defining competitive performance in the industry.

Historically, at least in the United States, there has been little evidence of increases in market concentration in the mutual fund industry. The largest mainstream funds and the smallest targeted funds have, however, gradually eroded the market share of actively managed midsize funds. Factors that seem to argue *for* greater industry concentration in the future come from the trend toward less sophisticated investors in taxable funds and mutual funds that are part of retirement packages. Economies of scale and brand-name concentration will advantage accounts battling for attention among the enormous number of funds vying for this business. Arguments *against* further concentration include shifts in performance track records and the role of mutual fund supermarkets in distribution. The supermarkets increase the relative marketing advantage of small funds. Moreover, it is almost impossible for the largest funds to outperform their benchmarks by significant amounts; specialized funds have an advantage in this effort.

In addition to promoting their performance (when favorable), mutual fund firms and securities broker/dealers have aggressively added such banking-type services as checking and cash management accounts, credit cards, and overdraft lines. They provide user-friendly, integrated account statements and tax reporting. Client contact is based on easy access by telephone, mail, and the internet.

Banks have similarly pushed aggressively into the mutual fund business, although they need to be wary of cannibalizing profitable banking clients. Securities firms and securities units of financial conglomerates have also increased their mutual fund activity, presumably with the view that this part of the securities industry is more capable of supporting significant, sustained returns than is wholesale investment banking, where competition has become cutthroat, capital intensive, and subject to a high degree of earnings instability. Insurance companies have also considered the mutual fund business a strong candidate for strategic development, especially in the face of competition in their traditional annuities business and the interpenetration that has emerged in some countries between the pension fund and mutual fund industries.

Competition in the mutual fund business thus covers a rich array of players, ranging from commercial banks and securities broker/dealers to specialized mutual fund firms, discount brokerages, insurance companies, and nonfinancial firms. Such incursions by strategic groups, each approaching the business from a different direction, tend to make markets hypercompetitive. This arrangement is the likely future competitive structure of the mutual fund industry, particularly in such large, integrated markets as the United States, Japan, and the eurozone.

The evidence nevertheless suggests an increase in concentration among mutual fund management firms and their fund families and fund complexes. **Table 5** shows that a disproportionate share of the net sales of funds appear to go to a small cohort of the largest management firms both in the United States and in Europe. This circumstance suggests that greater AUM concentration will occur down the road—presumably because of scale and scope economies in fund marketing and fund administration.

Table 5. Asset Management Industry Concentration, 2014

	Equity		Fixed Income	
	Proportion of Funds	Share of Net Sales	Proportion of Funds	Share of Net Sales
US-domiciled funds				
Largest	5%	53%	5%	57%
2nd largest	15	28	15	28
3rd largest	30	15	30	12
Smallest	50	4	50	3
Europe-domiciled funds				
Largest	5%	56%	5%	38%
2nd largest	15	29	15	24
3rd largest	30	13	30	21
Smallest	50	2	50	17

Note: Based on funds with positive net sales only.

Sources: Morningstar, BCG analysis, and Boston Consulting Group.

Comparative Regulation and Taxation of Mutual Funds

In the United States, regulations contain strict "fit and proper" criteria for management firms that sell mutual funds to the public and require extensive disclosure of pertinent information. That is, fund managers must be qualified and registered under the terms of the Investment Company Act of 1940, which outlines criteria for investment firms dealing with the public.

Under the National Securities Markets Improvement Act of 1996, the SEC is responsible for overseeing investment advisers with more than US$25 million of AUM. State regulators are responsible for investment advisers holding smaller amounts under management (such advisers had previously been co-regulated by the SEC). Large investment advisers falling under SEC jurisdiction account for about 95% of US AUM, although the vast majority of abusive practices and enforcement problems occur among the smaller firms.

The threat of regulatory action or civil liability lawsuits keeps the pressure on US mutual fund boards to take their obligations to investors seriously and to ensure that fund objectives are faithfully carried out. Some fund management firms, however, nominate individuals to serve as directors of a large number (sometimes a huge number) of funds managed by the firm, which raises questions about whether such directors can fulfill all their responsibilities to mutual fund investors. If they fail in their fiduciary responsibilities, they can expect to be the object of legal action brought by lawyers representing the investors as a class.

As noted previously, controversy has surrounded the fiduciary obligation of brokers that sell mutual funds (among other financial products). The brokerage industry argues "let the buyer beware" (*caveat emptor*); its opponents argue "let the seller beware" (*caveat venditor*). This debate continues even after the 2015 SEC decision to subject brokers to a fiduciary standard. It will no doubt be tested in future court decisions or resolved by legislative or regulatory action.

Virtually all pertinent information in the United States about the mutual fund industry is in the public domain and enjoys a high degree of transparency with respect to fund performance—as well as ample media coverage and vigorous competition among funds and fund managers. Thus, today's investors inhabit a generally fair and efficient market in which to make their asset choices. It is a good example of how regulation and competition can come together to serve the retail investor well.

In contrast to the United States, the rules governing the operation and distribution of mutual funds in Europe have traditionally been highly fragmented—a fragmentation scheduled to come to an end in the years ahead.

As of the mid-1980s, definitions of mutual funds varied from country to country in Europe, as did legal status and regulatory provisions. Door-to-door selling was forbidden in Belgium and Luxembourg, for example, and strictly regulated in Germany. In the United Kingdom, however, direct marketing was the norm. Market access to clients varied between the extremes of a high level of impenetrability to virtually complete openness.

The EU directive governing the operation and sale of mutual funds—Undertakings for the Collective Investment of Transferable Securities (UCITS)—came into force on 1 October 1989 after 15 years of negotiations. It specifies general rules for the kinds of investments that are appropriate for mutual funds and how they are to be sold. The regulatory requirements for fund management and certification are left to the home country of the fund management firm; specific rules governing the adequacy of disclosure and selling practices are left to the respective host countries.

Consequently, mutual funds that are duly established and monitored in any EU member country—and are in compliance with UCITS—can be sold without restriction to investors in national financial markets EU-wide. They can be promoted and advertised through local marketing networks and via direct mail so long as the selling requirements applicable in each country are met. Permissible investment vehicles include conventional equity and fixed-income securities and "synthetic" funds based on futures and options that are intended to deliver high performance and were not previously permitted in some financial centers (e.g., London).

Under UCITS, 90% of mutual fund assets must be invested in publicly traded companies, no more than 5% of the outstanding stock of any company may be owned by a mutual fund, and investment funds' borrowing rights are limited. Real estate funds, commodity funds, and money market funds are specifically excluded from UCITS.

Problems with UCITS have centered on differing marketing regulations among member countries. Although a UCITS II directive was proposed in the early 1990s to remove these obstacles, the EU Council of Ministers could not come to an agreement and the proposal was abandoned. In 1998, the UCITS III directive was proposed to address the marketing issues. Adopted in 2001, UCITS III gives mutual fund firms a "European passport" to sell anywhere in the EU. The UCITS IV directive, approved in 2009, specifies the sharing of information between member state regulatory authorities as well as the procedure for mutual fund mergers.

US mutual funds, in contrast, have operated in a comparatively coherent environment. For example, the federal income tax code requires mutual fund firms to report all income and capital gains to the Internal Revenue Service

(IRS)—there is normally no withholding at the source—and also requires individuals to self-report the same information in annual tax returns. Data reconciliation is undertaken by the IRS. Taxable fund income is subject to regular federal income tax rates, whereas capital gains and losses are recorded as they are incurred in mutual fund trading and net gains attributed to the mutual fund investor are taxed at the federal capital gains rates. Tax fraud, including the use of offshore accounts to evade taxes, is a criminal offense. States (and sometimes municipalities) similarly tend to tax mutual fund income and capital gains (and sometimes assets) at substantially lower rates than at the federal level.

Under the US Constitution, state and the federal governments cannot tax one another. So, a broad range of mutual funds invests in securities issued by state and local governments, with income exempt from federal tax and, usually, from tax imposed by the state in which a given security is issued. Similarly, the states do not tax income derived from federal government securities.

The US tax environment, although complex, provides its mutual fund industry with opportunities for product development (e.g., tax-efficient funds investing in municipal bonds and/or capital gains–oriented equities). The tax structure also imposes predictable compliance costs in terms of required tax reporting to the IRS and investor clients.

The European tax environment has been far more heterogeneous. The power of tax authorities stops at the national border, and—given the high tax rates on capital income in many EU countries—tax avoidance and evasion by investors is widespread. In light of intra-EU capital mobility, the euro, and the UCITS initiative, narrowing or eliminating intra-EU differentials in taxation of capital income and assets and establishing a coherent, equitable, and evasion-resistant tax environment are of continuing interest.

In the end, a financially integrated Europe will doubtless no more permit a haven for tax evaders than the US government permits a state to declare itself a federal tax haven. Indeed, substantial progress has been made, notably through EU and OECD initiatives to deal with tax evasion and from US pressure on Swiss banks and other intermediaries aiding and abetting tax evasion by US residents. The objective is routine reporting of assets and capital income by financial intermediaries abroad to the home-country tax authorities of the investor.

As previously noted, mutual funds have been less prone to malfeasance and disciplinary action by regulators than other parts of the financial system. Unfortunate exceptions include the "late-trading" and "market-timing" scandals of 2002–2003. In so-called late trading, mutual fund management firms allowed hedge funds to trade at their funds' close-of-market NAVs for several hours after the NAVs had been fixed until the next opening of the market. Hedge funds could thus trade in shares in the aftermarket or in foreign markets and then trade out of those positions at an assured profit by reselling to the mutual fund at the "stale" NAV.

This practice was akin to "betting on yesterday's horse race" and amounted to, in effect, stealing from ordinary investors. In return, the favored hedge funds would park "sticky" assets with in-house hedge funds run by the affected mutual funds' management firms. This scandal was a sorry spectacle indeed in an industry where fiduciary obligations and trust are paramount. It contravened US securities laws and ultimately cost the industry close to US$3 billion in fines and penalties. For some firms, such as Putnam (a unit of Marsh McLennan at the time), the reputational costs proved terminal.

A second mutual fund practice that, although not illegal, was unethical is market timing. The term sounds innocuous because funds are supposed to find the most (legally) advantageous time to trade on behalf of their investors. In the scandal, however, hedge funds and other large investors would trade actively in and out of mutual funds to take advantage of event-based or time zone–related profit windows in the market. This practice, which really should be called "time-zone arbitrage," is unfair because it increases the trading costs of mutual funds, which are paid by all investors through the expense ratio. These costs reduce returns to investors. Market timing also forces managers to hold more liquidity to accommodate large redemptions or inflows to be invested.

A third area of mutual fund controversy involves money market mutual funds (MMMFs) during the financial market crisis, particularly "prime" (as opposed to retail) MMMFs held by institutions. A run on MMMFs was triggered in 2008 by the Reserve Primary Fund, one of the pioneers in the industry, which held a material position in Lehman Brothers' short-term debt at the time of the firm's bankruptcy and was forced to "break the buck"—that is, redeem funds at less than par value. Given the threat of a massive run on MMMFs and the consequent threat to the commercial paper market, the US Treasury guaranteed the par values of all MMMFs. Like all crisis bailouts involving socialization of risks, this one came with strings attached—in this case, proposals to either force MMMF managers to hold capital against possible losses or mark MMMFs to market, perhaps both. These proposals were fiercely resisted by the mutual fund industry.

The debate came to a head in 2014, when the SEC announced that prime and municipal MMMFs sold to institutions had to be priced and transacted at a "floating" NAV. For these funds, "breaking the buck" thus became a nonissue. Moreover, during periods of extraordinary market stress, both retail and institutional prime and municipal MMMFs are allowed to charge shareholders liquidity fees, payable to the fund upon redemption, and apply redemption gates that temporarily halt all withdrawals. The rule exempts government and US Treasury money market mutual funds.

Finally, there continue to be controversial issues surrounding the performance of mutual funds and the creation of value, after fees, for retirement and nonretirement purposes. These issues concern time periods (length and choice of starting and ending dates) used in performance measurement, the choice of an appropriate benchmark (e.g., the S&P 500 Index versus the Russell 2000 Index), survivorship bias (a positive bias created as the worst performers disappear from the scene), risk adjustment of returns and calculation of the Sharpe ratio, and the size and structure of management fees and loads. Additional issues include 12b-1 charges (a US practice of charging sales fees to the investor) calibrated as annual return-equivalents, performance distribution over market cycles and relative to the sector mean, and persistence of outperformance. And finally, "What's in a name?" Does the fund name reflect the investment approach, or is there significant style drift?

Growth Challenges

The most pressing challenge facing the mutual fund sector today is the drag on growth triggered by the financial turbulence of 2007–2008. The crisis resulted in assets flowing out of actively managed mutual funds and investors switching funds both within and between fund complexes in rapid reaction to moves in the market. If active fund managers do not protect the investor in times of financial turbulence and, on the whole, do not outperform the market in favorable conditions, then the active management fees being charged are clearly excessive. As a result, index funds, including indexed exchange-traded funds (ETFs), look that much more attractive. **Figure 5**, **Table 6**, and **Table 7** show the gains made by index funds and ETFs relative to actively managed funds in recent years.

All the trends and developments have heightened the uncertainty for mutual fund managers. In each of the last three financial crises, the mutual fund industry suffered temporary AUM losses but after a year or so, AUM rebounded to previous AUM levels.

As noted, the mutual fund industry has a good fiduciary track record. And although there is a threat of increased regulation, regulation itself is clearly one of the industry's biggest advantages. Public oversight and supervision, in combination with the industry's self-regulation, have led to traditionally high levels of transparency on the part of mutual funds—arguably more transparency than is offered by any other form of financial intermediation.

Figure 5. Redirection of New US Fund Investments, 2007–2014 (cumulative flows in US$ billions)

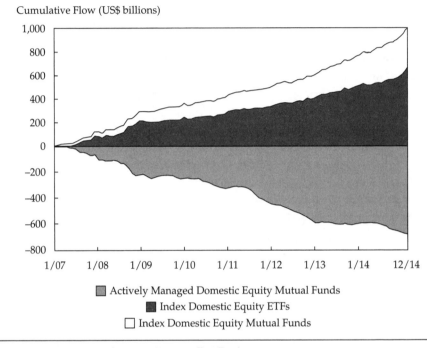

Source: 2015 Investment Company Institute Fact Book.

For both the near and the medium term, the four key growth issues in the mutual fund sector are private retirement savings, products and planning, emerging markets, and scale and internationalization.

Private Retirement Savings. As a result of changing demographics, increased private retirement savings will represent a major source of growth for mutual funds. The tendency to save more and retire later will spur growth in the industry. In a recent US survey, 75% of investors in mutual funds stated that their primary purpose in holding funds was retirement funding. In 2014, 36% of the assets in US mutual funds arose from formal retirement accounts—an amount exceeding US$4 trillion.

Moreover, the previously mentioned trend in pension funds away from DB plans and toward DC plans and the aging of the population in almost every developed country drive the need to set aside retirement savings.

In almost every country around the world, life expectancy is increasing and fewer workers will be funding retirees. Thus, paying for retirement at a rate that allows retirees to live with dignity will be a major problem

Table 6. New Cash Flows into US Index Funds, 2000–2014 (US$ billions)

Year	Domestic Equity	World Equity	Bond and Hybrid	Total
2000	21	2	2	26
2001	18	1	8	27
2002	17	2	7	25
2003	31	2	2	35
2004	28	6	7	40
2005	11	8	8	28
2006	14	11	8	33
2007	28	17	16	61
2008	31	−6	10	35
2009	25	4	27	56
2010	14	19	24	58
2011	18	17	20	55
2012	15	16	29	59
2013	52	28	34	114
2014	61	38	49	148

Source: 2015 Investment Company Institute Fact Book.

everywhere. Mutual fund management companies that exploit this opportunity will rank among the industry winners. The solution to the retirement dilemma will inevitably involve encouraging more savings at an earlier age and the education of employees, an area in which mutual funds can and should play a leading role. Filling the gap in savings would be not only a tremendous business opportunity but also a way for the mutual fund industry to make a significant contribution to society.

Mutual funds are a natural component of a retirement system. They offer transparency along many dimensions—in particular, with respect to valuing the collection of fund assets—as well as flexibility in design and the ability to change the mix of funds. This last factor allows participants to achieve goals as their particular circumstances change.

Mutual funds should be encouraged to take a leading role in educating the public and policymakers on the need to save for retirement and the need for incentives to encourage such saving. Overall, the industry should be an advocate for tax policy that encourages saving for retirement. It should also be a strong advocate for portability in pensions, both within and between countries.

Table 7. Growth of ETFs, 2003–2014

Year	Total Net Assets (US$ billions)			Number of ETFs
	1940 Act ETFs[a]	Non-1940 Act ETFs[b]	Total	
2003	151	—	151	119
2004	226	2	228	152
2005	296	5	301	204
2006	408	15	423	359
2007	580	29	608	629
2008	496	36	531	728
2009	703	75	777	797
2010	891	101	992	923
2011	939	109	1,048	1,134
2012	1,217	120	1,337	1,194
2013	1,611	64	1,675	1,294
2014	1,918	57	1,974	1,411

[a]The funds in this category are registered under the Investment Company Act of 1940.
[b]The funds in this category are not registered under the Investment Company Act of 1940 and invest primarily in commodities, currencies, and futures.
Source: 2015 Investment Company Institute Fact Book.

Given the demographics, there will continue to be large inflows into the private pension system—inflows that should exceed outflows for many years to come. The mutual fund industry should benefit from this dynamic so long as it develops in a way that both encourages the use of its (attractive) investment products and serves an economic purpose.

Innovation, Products, and Planning. First, it should use existing distribution channels and establish new ones (third party or direct) to offer mutual fund–related products and services. A large part of the success of mutual fund firms will depend on designing products and services that meet the needs of pension fund participants.

Second, although product design is important, the real breakthrough will be in advising participants how to plan for retirement: what savings rate and asset allocation are appropriate in light of the participant's wealth, predicted income, and planned retirement age. This approach requires advice at every stage of a participant's working life but particularly at retirement. Here, mutual fund firms can provide such pension services as annuities, financial planning advice, record keeping, and related services.

Third, the industry should develop products that are designed to meet retirement needs. Although advice on the right product mix is important, some products can be either a replacement or a starting point for individual choice. One product class that could start this process is a stable of life-cycle or target-date funds. These funds serve as an asset mix vehicle for pension holders at different stages of their working lives and retirement. The guidance life-cycle and target-date funds provide is important. The concept and its implementation are still relatively new and need to be refined.

Finally, not only do pension fund participants differ in wealth and planned retirement age, but they also differ in their attitudes toward risk. Products should be developed that serve these different clienteles. At a minimum, a product with an inflation-protected return should be offered.

Innovation has always been one of the mutual fund industry's strong suits. Traditionally, the industry has tended to think in terms of "product" in hopes of attracting capital and making a profit. Mutual fund firms take the world of securities and slice and dice them any one of several ways to form mutual funds.

Designing active funds generally involves determining areas in which the fund company has special ability, funds that will have market appeal, or funds needed to fill out a product line to compete with other mutual fund families. The industry focuses on delivering a process rather than a product.

Value can be added by offering financial planning at different levels— partly as a way to sell product but also as a useful tool in itself. More and more firms have financial software packages aimed at delivering a useful product to clients and helping them plan. This approach includes everything from full-scale private banking for wealthy clients to tax planning for small-scale clients. Components of viable mutual fund strategies include the following.

First, the mutual fund industry has traditionally done a good job of designing funds that partition securities according to type (growth, value, income, small- or large-company securities, etc.). Funds are also frequently designed to appeal to a set of tastes or social goals (e.g., "green" or "sustainability" funds, energy funds, or funds that avoid socially undesirable products, such as tobacco). A fund complex needs to consider the economics of these funds as well as the labels. For example, do people hold sustainability funds because they feel good about holding stocks in such funds or are these stocks projected to have a high return because of socially responsible business practices?

Second, fund complexes are starting to think about funds not simply as an aggregation of securities by characteristic but, rather, as an aggregation of securities to satisfy customer needs. The ability to expand the types of funds offered by emphasizing investor needs will be a major engine for growth. New products designed to meet investor needs include lifestyle and target-date funds, absolute return funds, inflation-protected funds, and structured funds.

Third, new products to satisfy investors' financial needs and risk tolerances will stimulate financial services designed to help investors pick the right funds and make appropriate asset allocations. This development will involve a change in the industry, with fund complexes delivering both a service and the products to accompany that service.

Fourth, fund families run the gamut, from big complexes that offer a large number of mutual funds covering almost every conceivable division of the market to boutique complexes offering a small number of funds, which tend to concentrate on a specific area of the market. Large fund complexes can and should deliver advisory services. Smaller, specialized fund complexes will be under increased pressure to find a mechanism that allows them to become part of an organizational structure that can meet investor needs.

Finally, as "process" becomes more important to the industry, the value chain of an organization—and its entire management, from advisory to distribution outlets—will assume far greater prominence in efforts to gain and maintain competitive advantage. Investment management firms with a retail banking network at their disposal have a built-in advantage in selling financial products based on advice; products sold through third-party distribution channels are much more volatile and dependent on short-term performance criteria.

Emerging Markets. Emerging markets continue to represent a significant growth opportunity for the mutual fund sector of the asset management industry—as a source of both new products and new customers. Rapid expected growth in wealth and a tremendous savings capacity in countries like China and India are obvious. As the share of emerging economies in global economic output keeps increasing, these markets will become an essential source of demand for investment products and management.

The challenge is that competition between US and European funds and funds domiciled in Asia, the Middle East, and Latin America is likely to increase. The cause is the desire by local regulators to promote the development of a local mutual fund industry that replicates the success of the US industry and the EU's UCITS provisions—at times, with the tacit support of global fund management firms.

Those investment fund firms that figure out how to acquire the necessary knowledge to exploit the growth opportunities offered by emerging markets as outlets and conduits for new products and new customers will rank among the industry winners.

First, the industry should propose solutions that promote the cost efficiency and competitiveness of European and US mutual funds. It should promote their attractiveness as models for effective regulation and risk-adjusted performance.

Second, mutual fund complexes should decide whether to establish a presence in any emerging market where competitive advantage is not immediately self-evident. If they decide to enter a market, they should consider such market penetration tactics as joint marketing arrangements, partnerships, or outsourcing to local players as a means of safeguarding against domestic political uncertainties and economic vagaries. Funds must be aware of and overcome cultural and institutional difficulties by emphasizing objective, neutral product offerings and service provision. They must apply a global approach, combined with local skills and expertise, with a view to extending the mutual fund franchise into targeted emerging markets.

Third, part of an approach to emerging markets is to engage in practices that protect against liquidity issues, such as massive asset outflows and other disruptive financial influences. The more globally dispersed a fund complex's investors, the greater the competitive advantage.

Fourth, mutual funds should try to expand into emerging markets that are close to home, possibly with cultural and linguistic affinities (e.g., Eastern Europe for European fund companies and Latin America for North American ones).

Finally, mutual fund firms should roll out their global investment management and distribution platforms and interface them with local outlets, including promising emerging markets for subscription and redemption purposes. This approach involves applying and, where necessary, adapting the in-house savings concept and other advisory mechanisms to the local market.

Scale and Internationalization. As the scale and internationalization of the mutual fund industry grow, challenges will arise because mutual fund products are not standardized—for a number of reasons, particularly tax policy.

A key determinant of the success (or failure) of internationalization efforts is which model will prevail: the bank-affiliated mutual fund model widely seen in Europe or the more independent mutual fund provider seen in the United States (Fidelity, Franklin Templeton, etc.). The latter model is less subject to conflicts of interest. Still, opinion remains divided over the best operating method for achieving a competitive advantage in a climate of growing internationalization.

For some, full integration with a captive distribution channel is the preferred method. Others opt for third-party distribution and open architecture.

Still others believe that distribution via bank channels is at least as important as distribution through independent channels.

Those investment fund companies that have already built and integrated the necessary asset management platforms (based on appropriately applied and flexible IT processes, sales outlets, and advisory services) to accommodate scale and internationalization will be among the industry's leaders for several reasons.

First, the industry's competitive landscape has changed. There is a need to understand the reasons why some sectors of the mutual fund industry have experienced less growth than others and to identify the major factors behind this slowdown.

Second, it would help industry growth if mutual fund products were standardized, particularly in the European market, which remains prone to fragmentation. Concentration among major players has occurred, especially with respect to new funds, and concentration has occurred among those players that are operating across markets.

Third, industry players need to assess whether their fund platforms and volumes are scalable, particularly when consolidation enters the picture. Size and scale together are good for the organizations that have the necessary resources and integrated platforms. Small players that cannot achieve large scale will probably face a hard time entering the market and succeeding—or be acquired by larger firms

Fourth, the value proposition of those companies that succeed needs to be identified. For example, cross-border firms probably recovered better from the 2007–08 financial crisis than their locally based counterparts in terms of AUM.

Key Risk Challenges

For both the near and the medium term, the four key risk challenges in the mutual fund sector are market risk, valuation and credit risk, regulatory risk, and operational risk.

Market Risk. Market risk centers on financial market instability and heightened volatility—as exemplified by the collapse of Lehman Brothers in September 2008. The fall of Lehman Brothers resulted in a loss of confidence in both financial markets and investment funds and slowed mutual fund industry growth. This instability was accentuated by investors switching between mutual funds as they chased short-term performance at the expense of continuity and stability. Many investors, selling at or near the bottom, missed the strong stock market recovery.

In a sense, mutual funds had been oversold before the financial crisis. The diminished industry growth was reflected in both a decline in AUM (which subsequently recovered) and the reduced number of households owning mutual funds (which has yet to recover). Separating the winners from the losers among mutual fund firms in this harsher market environment will be (1) performance and alpha generation and (2) treating clients fairly by not misrepresenting products and by helping them understand the risks and returns of products.

First, investor confidence should be restored. Achieving this goal involves providing both better "education" about the purpose of mutual funds and better and more easily understood data on the performance of funds. Mutual funds provide investors with the ability to share in the profitability of the capital markets with lower transaction costs, more complete and less expensive diversification, better professional management, and more transparent and audited results than can be obtained by owning individual securities or through other financial intermediaries.

Second, education should start at the aggregate level. Programs and reports should be developed that present in easily understood form a clear picture of the aggregate performance of mutual funds. This approach involves performance statistics for all funds, perhaps disaggregated by country and type (growth, income, etc.). In addition, performance must be seen from the perspective of a long-term investor, not that of a short-term trader. Because mutual funds offer low-cost diversification, good performance, and the ability to overcome short-term movements in market levels, they are a preferred instrument for investors planning for the future. Investors need to be educated about the favorable risk characteristics of mutual funds and shown that simply chasing returns or buying a small portfolio of stocks cannot produce results as favorable as those produced by owning mutual funds.

Part of this process has to be the development of appropriate and easily understood benchmarks by which to judge mutual fund performance. External information providers (e.g., Morningstar) produce benchmarks for the investor. It is important that the industry play a role in the development and dissemination of benchmarks. If it does not do so, it will find itself judged by criteria that may or may not be relevant. Only if the industry sets realistic and appropriate standards can it be assured that at least some third-party providers will supply appropriate criteria for judging both the industry and individual funds.

Third, the industry needs to develop greater transparency and consistency. Although the industry has done a good job of creating transparent return data, work remains to be done. Marketing and sales personnel must do a careful and objective job of presenting mutual fund information. If a good product is portrayed inaccurately, the purchaser may be dissatisfied. Controls need to be exercised on all marketing and sales materials.

Fourth, switching has both pros and cons. The ability of mutual fund investors to switch their investments at low or no cost between funds in the same complex or between funds in different complexes is both a major advantage of and a hindrance for mutual funds. It is an advantage because it has appropriate appeal for the serious investor, who will want, and should have the right, to switch funds across types of investments. Switching is logical and has an economic rationale as an investor's circumstances change because of health, age, or employment. It is also logical because market movements may result in an investor's having too large a percentage of the portfolio invested in a category of funds that has done well over a long period. These types of trades should not be discouraged; the short-term trader is hurting not only himself, however, but also other fund shareholders. The trader who tries to exploit short-term returns imposes costs on longer-term holders of mutual funds. Such switches can be especially costly in times of crisis in the financial markets.

Fifth, new solutions are needed. Mechanisms must be developed that penalize frequent traders without imposing high costs on long-term investors. Measures are needed to handle the liquidity and dilution problems that occur during crises. The impact of such solutions as entry and exit fees, switching fees for intervals shorter than a specified period, and swing pricing[9] must be considered and IT systems developed to study and implement these alternatives.

The actively managed mutual fund industry needs to position itself with respect to increased competition from index funds, ETFs, hedge funds, and money market funds. The risk–return characteristics of each of these instruments should be examined, and the appropriateness of each instrument for different types of investors analyzed. For example, ETFs may be a superior product for the frequent trader but not for the longer-term investor. The existence of ETFs might even help traditional mutual funds by siphoning off frequent traders.

Finally, in examining performance and the risk–return characteristics of individual products, appropriate measures of tail risk and value at risk (VaR) must be developed. These models, properly implemented, can be used to understand worst-case scenarios and can serve as a useful addition to

---

[9]The volatility that exists in the financial markets can be seen easily when the price of a certain security undergoes rapid changes in value. These sharp shifts are often referred to as a swing. For example, it is not uncommon to see a major index swing from negative territory to positive territory just prior to the market close (see www.investopedia.com/terms/s/swing. asp#ixzz3ge51LqWT). Fees and commissions may be tailored to the swing.

mean–variance analysis. These measures should be incorporated into investment management systems.

Valuation and Credit Risk. Valuation and credit risks center on price discontinuities and disparities, which pose problems for valuation and credit assessment and may cause the failure of some instruments held in mutual fund portfolios. An additional lesson from the crisis is that massive new fund flows in a market with increasing spreads can lead to significant dilution effects in a "single-NAV universe," damaging fund performance.

Ideally, a bid–offer NAV would mitigate most of the risk impact; instead, such measures as swing pricing and antidilution levies have been introduced, which may prove ineffective.

Liquidity risk and its management is another area that has received a great deal of attention. As certain asset classes turn less liquid, managers may be forced to sell liquid assets when investors redeem funds, leaving the remaining investors with the less attractive and more illiquid assets. If proven business and IT models to manage and/or monitor liquidity and investor behavior are not in place, the risk of acting too late and being forced into selling becomes all the greater. This risk carries with it significant financial and reputational consequences.

Those mutual fund firms that have business and IT models for measuring and monitoring valuation and credit risk and apply the models correctly are likely to rank among the industry's winners. The first steps in meeting this challenge are to identify a reliable and transparent valuation process and to develop models for determining prices of nonpublicly traded securities as well as models for publicly traded securities when markets are closed. Closely aligned is the development of internal credit models. Independent credit ratings are now required in the United States. Both valuation and credit models require the development of procedures to monitor the implementation of the modeling process and to assess the accuracy of the results over time.

Systems must also be developed to monitor risk control measures and compliance functions at each stage of the transaction process and management chain—implementation from front office to back office, distribution, asset management, private wealth, and advisory services. If risk is controlled in the investment process but not at the final point of sale, the risk control function cannot be properly implemented. To ensure consistency, straight-through processing and algorithmic trading can be used. In short, risk management strategy and IT solutions must involve determining and ensuring the integrity of the data, models, and processes—which must be done at every stage of the investment distribution and sales chain.

Regulatory Risk. As previously noted, the increased pace of regulatory reform since 2008 has created uncertainty and dislocation. For the investment management industry, the regulatory and compliance challenges in the years ahead will be unprecedented. Among the many strategic, tactical, systemic, and operational changes that need to be understood are the new regulatory framework and demands of the landmark Dodd–Frank Act of 2010 in the United States and AIFMD, MiFID (conduct of business), Packaged Retail Investment Products, Solvency II, and UCITS IV in the European Union. Internationally, the new tax rules and standards are embodied primarily in IFRS 9, Financial Instruments.

As noted, regulation is both good and bad: It increases the mutual fund industry's credibility, but it also produces uncertainty about what rules are going to need to be followed. Winners in this sphere will be those mutual fund management firms that recognize early the importance of internal regulatory compliance procedures and mechanisms to deal with the challenge of increased regulation.

The mutual fund industry should be encouraged to find common ground with regulators on compliance issues and legal requirements. Good regulation is advantageous to the industry. Furthermore, becoming part of the regulatory process provides lead-time in adjusting to future legislation and self-regulatory initiatives.

Despite the fact that the mutual fund industry offers perhaps the most transparent investment product available to the general public, funds should (1) tighten consumer protection and fiduciary standards, (2) exercise caution in decision making, and (3) clarify or dispel uncertainty surrounding new regulations.

It is also in the industry's interest to simplify its structure. To add both transparency and simplicity, the industry should advocate the standardizing of tax requirements, lower externally imposed administrative burdens and restrictions, and reduce the complexity of mutual fund structures.

Finally, the mutual fund industry should recognize that extending regulation to the hedge fund industry following the financial crisis could pose a potential risk if mutual funds become more like hedge funds (or vice versa) and the distinctions between the two are blurred.

Operational Risk. Operational risk today includes risk associated with mutual fund liability for investor obligations—as part of the risk arising from execution of a mutual fund firm's business functions. This concept is broadly focused on the risks arising from the people, systems, and processes through which a fund management firm operates.

Operational risk also includes fraud risk, legal risk, and physical or environmental risk. A widely used definition of operational risk states that it comprises the risks of loss resulting from inadequate or failed internal processes, people, and systems and from external events. For mutual funds, this definition would seem to mandate the following: (1) accepting that people, processes, and systems are imperfect and that errors can arise at every level of internal operations as well as at the interface with the public; (2) assessing the size of the acceptable loss for operational risk; (3) committing an adequate level of expenditure to develop monitoring and control systems for ensuring that the desired level of risk is not exceeded; and (4) recognizing that eliminating any chance of loss would be prohibitively expensive, if not impossible.

Cost-Related Challenges

For the near and the medium term, the four key challenges concerning cost issues in the mutual fund sector are industry concentration, external outsourcing, fee shrinkage, and cost and profit allocation. **Figure 6** shows that US-managed equity mutual fund expense ratios average around 95 bps, although changes in the shares of different types of funds have increased the weight of cheaper funds and led to a gradual decline in overall expenses charged to investors.

Figure 6. Expense Ratios of US Equity Mutual Funds, 2000–2014

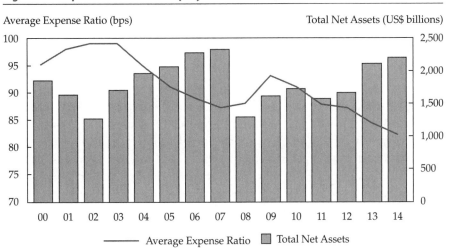

Notes: Based on a fixed sample of share classes. Average expense ratio measured as a percentage of asset-weighted averages.

Source: 2015 Investment Company Institute Fact Book.

Industry Concentration. When considering costs, one must take into account the mutual fund industry's increasingly concentrated structure, which arises from the market power of the largest players and the increasing costs of entering the industry. The economies of scale for both individual funds and fund complexes remain incompletely understood. Studies indicate that, at least in Europe, mutual fund managers have different cost structures. Some have lower IT backbone costs but higher marginal costs—attributable to lower efficiency and scalability. Others have higher IT backbone costs but lower marginal costs because of investments in efficiency and scalability.

A mutual fund firm can either team up with an operational outsourcing partner or invest in an in-house platform and organization. Either way, the key issues include the following:

- Economies of scale at the fund level and fund-complex level are not as well understood as they might be. At the level of the individual fund, there is a trade-off between the negative impact of increased fund size on investment strategy and the scale benefits of larger AUM and transaction volume for costs, the ability to hire better managers, and name recognition in the marketplace.

- For fund families, there may be tension between economies and diseconomies of scale, but the advantages of larger size for fund complexes are more compelling than the advantages at the fund level (professional trading desks, reputational recognition, and sales and distribution functions)—although, at some point, problems of span of control, managing bigger organizations, and supervising the actions of a large number of employees may overtake the advantages of size.

- Given the advantages of size, particularly at the fund-family level, increased concentration in the mutual fund industry is likely to occur. Regarding the last point, concentration of fund families has proceeded rapidly, notably in the United States and Europe. The advantage of large size, together with the increases in the cost of market entry, has resulted in a reduction in the number of mutual funds. The largest mutual fund families need to monitor the impact of size on costs and simultaneously avoid monopolistic behavior, or they may face the threat of regulation.

In contrast to those in the United States, funds in Europe have structural barriers to harvesting the full benefit of scale economies. Technical and fiscal barriers continue to impede the free and unrestricted flow of mutual funds across borders, and funds are fragmented by legal restrictions on cross-border sales and by tax regimes in different countries. These frictions need to be addressed in the context of UCITS IV (mergers of funds, master-feeder funds, single "passports" for fund managers).[10]

Outsourcing. Outsourcing poses both challenges and opportunities for mutual funds. As in the case of pension funds, functions that can be outsourced include distribution, back-office operations, IT, and portfolio management. Both the quality of service and the cost of monitoring need to be considered before outsourcing.

Outsourcing solutions must be able to integrate state-of-the-art technology with strong business-specific knowledge and deliver top-of-the-line performance and uninterrupted operations—all centered on reliable and flexible management tools and operational workflow systems that focus on quality processing. Creating in-house systems based on "open architecture" as a blended approach may be sensible for (1) determining where outsourcing might make sense, given a firm's competitive advantages with respect to special skills or knowledge that an outside supplier does not have and what functions and information are proprietary and should not be transferred; (2) monitoring the performance of outsourced functions, including metrics and systems to continuously track and measure the quality of important outsourced functions; and (3) examining the balance between the costs and benefits of outsourcing. All these processes require IT solutions that, based on the individual investment management firm's business requirements, can assist in evaluating and monitoring outsourced functions.

Fee Shrinkage. Regulatory action, market competition, and asset management firm restructuring continue to reduce investor costs, including fees. Can fees, pressed by competition from index funds and indexed ETFs, shrink to the degree that investment is no longer justified in activities that are central to the future of the industry?

When the markets decline and fee pressure tends to be greatest, the first thing that investment fund firms often do is jettison services they will need in the long run—particularly, education of staff and clients as well as IT and analytical control functions—at a time when they are needed most. Managers tend to cut costs where they can in the short run and not worry about the long-term implications of doing business without these activities.

The industry must educate the public not only to examine fees but also to look beyond fees to performance. Given a fixed level of management performance, higher fees mean lower returns to investors. Better investment performance before fees, however, can result in a fund offering higher returns to investors even if its fees are higher than competitors' fees.

---

[10]Several guides to the UCITS IV are available—for example, www.lavenpartners.com/wp-content/uploads/2014/12/Laven-Definitive-Guidebook-to-UCITS-IV-Funds.pdf.

Nevertheless, fees in the active fund management industry have declined and are likely to continue to decline over time. This trend means that firm managers must control costs better and price products appropriately. Cost control systems will have to be designed to increase flexibility, not only over time but also in response to changes in inflows and outflows of individual fund complexes.

Cost and Profit Allocation. Companies that manage multiple mutual funds and/or multiple products often find it difficult to define the cost and profit of a particular fund, which creates problems related to cost allocation and assessment. Costs must be allocated reasonably to ensure fair treatment of investors, as well as for gauging entry and exit charges of swing-pricing elements.

Fund families need to develop robust models of cost allocation. The distinction between marginal and average costing is important in the mutual fund business because so many costs are joint costs. The marginal cost of adding a fund to a complex is low, and on that basis, a particular fund may look profitable. This approach can easily lead to a situation in which each fund more than covers its marginal cost but the fund complex does not cover its total cost.

Costs are marginal (variable) only with respect to a particular decision. Models need to be developed that not only measure the marginal cost of any decision but also determine whether that decision covers both the marginal cost and a rational allocation of joint costs. Thus, investment management systems need to be developed that allow the alternative cost structure of any decision to be evaluated.

Cost savings can be achieved in several areas. The levels of automation and STP applications within the mutual fund industry in general are arguably too low. Inefficiencies and the potential for cost savings are most apparent in the cross-border distribution of funds. The growing importance of both open and guided architecture exacerbates the operational costs for fund families and, ultimately, for investors.

Increasing the level of automation in back-office operations offers opportunities for fund managers to control both costs and risks. All key players along the value chain, especially fund distributors, have opportunities to harvest the benefits of automation. Part of cost allocation and profit attribution hinges on development of better performance measurement techniques. What should be the proper way to measure performance? Should it be on an absolute basis, relative to a peer group of products, or relative to index funds?

A growing body of evidence shows that past performance of mutual funds is somewhat predictive of future performance. There is also strong evidence that investors follow performance and place more assets into funds that have done well in the past one to three years whereas they remove money from funds that have done poorly. This strategy creates problems for poorly performing funds because their diminished size results in an increase in expense ratios and exacerbates the problem of reversing poor performance. Yet, large amounts of new money flowing into a mutual fund can create problems in investing the money even as it results in the spreading of fixed costs.

The mutual fund management industry needs to prepare for still further pressure on fees. Active managers, in particular, are under fee pressure from index funds and ETFs, from government regulation, and from alternative investments. **Figure 7** shows the compound annual growth rate (CAGR) versus net revenue margins for active funds and passive funds for 2010–2014. Passive index funds and ETFs guarantee "beta" returns for low fees, whereas alternatives provide the opportunity to access "alpha" returns at high fees. So, active mutual funds that charge high fees and produce little (or negative) alpha but plenty of beta are caught in the middle. And there seems to be a certain amount of convergence, with some active funds cutting fees and producing market returns and some passive funds and ETFs promising "index plus" returns, using sector selection approaches, and charging higher fees for the added value.

Figure 7. Growth vs. Margins for Active vs. Passive Funds, 2010–2014

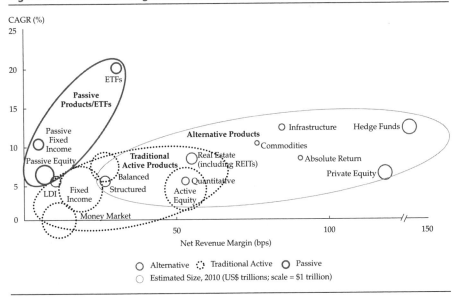

Note: Size of bubble is proportional to estimated AUM for 2010. LDI = liability-driven investing.

Source: Boston Consulting Group, "Global Asset Management 2014" (http://www.slideshare.net/TheBostonConsultingGroup/global-asset-management-2014).

5. The Alternative Assets Sector

For the purposes of this book, the alternative assets sector is defined as largely made up of two components: hedge funds and private equity funds. Some other asset classes, such as real estate and commodities, are usually considered to be alternative. Here, the hedge fund industry is emphasized because of its global growth and its size in terms of assets under management and the performance and regulatory issues that confront the industry. In addition to wealthy individuals, institutions have become large investors in both types of alternatives, although high fees and disclosure problems have moderated their participation of late.

Hedge funds are a type of special-purpose investment vehicle administered by a professional management firm. They are usually structured as limited partnerships or limited liability companies. Hedge fund firms may be independent entities, or they may be "captive" funds managed by units of universal banks (i.e., full-service investment banks) or financial conglomerates. They differ from mutual funds in that they can take long or short positions in a range of asset classes and can use leverage to enhance returns for hedge fund investors. Global hedge fund growth, which reached US$2.25 trillion in AUM at the end of 2014, is depicted in **Figure 8**.

Hedge funds tend to be open ended, with investors purchasing the shares from and selling the shares to the fund manager rather than another

Figure 8.   Hedge Fund Industry Growth, 2000–2014

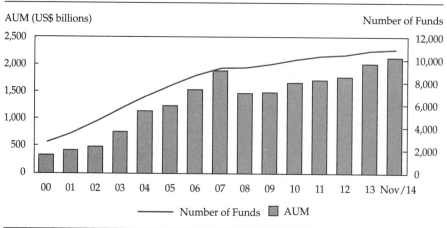

Source: Eurekahedge.

shareholder. Unlike traditional mutual funds, hedge fund investments and redemptions are usually permitted only at specified times—say, quarterly—and on the basis of calculated NAVs (net of fees and expenses). Hedge funds may close to new investors at the discretion of the managers.

Historically, hedge fund investors have consisted of wealthy families and individuals as well as institutions and have been relatively lightly regulated, sidestepping rules governing other types of managed funds with respect to their investment strategies and how they can be structured. In the United States, hedge funds come under the Investment Company Act of 1940. They are often registered in such tax havens as Switzerland, Singapore, and the Cayman Islands. Since the financial crisis of 2007–2008, hedge funds have come under increased regulation, particularly in the United States and Europe.

Hedge funds may or may not *hedge*. The classic model of a hedge fund is one that invests in long positions in assets that the manager thinks will rise in price and short positions in those thought likely to fall—a "long–short" strategy. This strategy may or may not be market neutral—that is, balanced so that the overall fund is insensitive to market movements. This model persists, but it is only one of many hedge fund strategies, and some strategies, unlike the long–short strategy, may not involve hedging.

Funds following "absolute return" strategies try to achieve a positive return regardless of overall market direction. Other forms include multi-strategy managed futures funds, global macro funds, fixed-income arbitrage funds, event-driven funds, equity market-neutral funds, emerging-market funds, dedicated short bias funds, and convertible arbitrage funds. There are also funds of funds, which claim to have the expertise to distinguish successful from unsuccessful hedge funds.

Hedge funds are an expensive way to have assets managed. The common hedge fund fee structure is 1.5%–2% annually on the NAV plus 20% of gains relative to a benchmark or other criterion, but with such participation fees often limited by "high-water marks."[11] Funds of funds typically invest in 20–25 hedge funds and add another fee, amounting typically to 1.5% on top of the underlying hedge fund fees, so that in many cases, the two sets of fees sum to 3.5% in annual fees plus 20% of gains.

Hedge fund managers tend to invest in their own funds, which suggests they have substantial skin in the game and aligns their interests with outside investors—all of which should reduce agency problems. Still, managers of large hedge funds can do well just on fees net of expenses.

---

[11]A high-water mark is a previous level of NAV that must be surpassed before performance fees are payable.

Expenses, moreover, are sometimes charged to the fund investors rather than to the manager, so the manager gets the whole fee. And the high expense levels can make beating market benchmarks difficult. Over the five years ended 30 April 2015, an investment in an index of equity hedge funds returned 4.83% a year, while the S&P 500 Index earned 14.31%. Through the financial crisis, however, hedge funds outperformed the S&P 500 and appear to be doing so again during the balance of 2015.

Hedge funds suffered a precipitous decline during the crisis years of 2007–2008, which is attributable to both the collapse of asset values (suggesting a lack of hedging against extreme events) and net redemptions of invested funds. Hedge fund AUM grew at a moderate pace thereafter, and the role of funds of funds diminished decisively and perhaps permanently.

Given the nature of the hedge fund industry, a substantial number of new hedge funds are launched every year and an equally substantial number are closed down, which makes measuring overall industry performance problematic.

Areas of Concern

In the wake of the global financial crisis, the hedge fund industry has made a concerted effort to restore investor confidence while dealing with intensified competition from several quarters and formulating a constructive set of responses to the increased regulatory pressure—some of which remains highly uncertain—that inevitably follows financial trauma. Much of the emphasis will have to be on improved transparency at all levels—products, processes, costs, and compliance—and a fundamental reconsideration by top management of these issues as sources of competitive advantage rather than purely defensive measures.

A particular area of concern is operational risk. Legal and regulatory risks are part of this mosaic. Operational risk issues reached their peak in the Bernie Madoff and Bear Stearns episodes, which showed the need for serious external audits by firms exposed to high levels of reputational risk.[12] Also needed are stress testing for both liquidity and earnings streams, reconsidering the structure of incentives, and dealing with the problem of risk aggregation in its transmission to senior managers and boards.

Needed are a good dose of common sense alongside traditional and proprietary risk modeling. Equally important are (1) disciplined cost accounting,

---

[12]Madoff turned his wealth management business into a massive Ponzi scheme. Bear Sterns had a highly leveraged balance sheet consisting of many illiquid and potentially worthless assets, including two subprime mortgage loans, which led to the rapid diminution of investor and lender confidence.

an area in which firms have often been found wanting in their rush to boost assets under management, and (2) operating leverage because of high fixed costs but variable revenues, trading costs, and uncertainty about the importance of economies of scale.

Given the difficulty of persistent outperformance in returns in any business structure, including hedge funds, costs are a critical competitive element and require imaginative outsourcing, application of world-class technology, and in some cases, serious conversations with clients about appropriate fee structures. Asset management has bright growth prospects worldwide. But unless risk and efficiency are addressed more effectively than in the past at a given firm, its competitors may be the main beneficiary of that growth.

Hedge funds and other alternative asset managers able to meet these challenges in the face of stiff, nontraditional competition are likely to be the most prominent winners. Business as usual is unlikely to produce the kind of growth, risk profile, or operating efficiency that hedge funds have enjoyed in the past.

Before the crisis, alternative asset management was quite different from what it is today. Businesses were able to survive with high cost structures. Now, we are seeing a need to control costs and a need to be transparent within the organization regarding the nature of the products being sold and the magnitude of the costs necessary to offer those products.

For the alternative asset management business, as well as the industry as a whole, the most pressing challenge is the loss of investor confidence resulting from the financial crisis. In addition, there is increased competition from low-cost providers, including "liquid alternative" providers, which claim to deliver hedge fund–like returns without the liquidity limitations of traditional hedge funds. Managers also face increased government regulation and intervention in the markets.

The opportunity for growth lies with those enterprises that are most able to meet these challenges by providing transparency to their clients, their stakeholders, and in particular, their regulators. Those that can meet these challenges will be the most effective in the future. Specifically, the industry's challenges can be grouped into three categories: growth, risk management, and cost control.

Growth

The expected growth in the hedge fund industry comes with challenges. The ability to adapt to change is key to survival. A significant increase in competition is coming from low-cost providers, which will necessitate a repositioning of the product mix for most of the asset management business. The low-cost providers depend on economies of scale, and the question arises whether and to what extent existing product offerings are scalable. Finally, how to correctly position the product mix in this new business environment must be considered.

The first and most obvious challenge is to identify solutions that address legitimate client concerns arising from the global financial crisis. Hedge fund management companies need to focus on such solutions and putting them in the market. Risk management solutions directed to the retail customer base are an example of a product that should be offered by most asset management firms.

One of the most common complaints of retail customers is that they must pay their investment advisers a fee when their accounts have not risen in value over a period that has been difficult for markets. Part of the response is education; investors do not always know what market returns have been or may not relate their own experience to that of other market participants. The most important point is to explain the necessity to save and invest for the long run, which will contain periods of good and bad performance. Part of the responsibility of the asset management business is to rebuild customer confidence, and improving operational transparency is a necessary part of that process.

Hedge fund distribution channels have been dramatically affected by the global financial crisis because major regulatory changes ensued in all financial jurisdictions. Hedge fund firms need to assess how the product mix should be adapted to address these changes. In addition, demographic changes in developed and developing markets have altered patterns of investing and saving. So, the product mix needs to be adapted to meet this new reality.

New markets for hedge funds have developed in the last several years. Commodity-rich emerging markets and the growth of sovereign wealth funds around the world represent new markets and new opportunities for hedge fund firms. The question is whether existing firms will be able to adapt to serve these markets or whether their place will be taken by new, more specialized enterprises.

Increased Competition. An important development in the last five years has been the dramatic increase in competition for funds from low-cost providers, particularly traditional index funds and index ETFs, which have adapted to many different investor clienteles. This competition represents a significant challenge to the revenue base of more traditional hedge fund firms. It is vitally important to consider precisely what competitive advantage a given product has and to highlight it. In addition, low-cost competitors underline the importance of cost containment, consolidation of product lines internally, and cost control with respect to external service providers.

The industry needs to challenge the assumption that increased scale alone will decrease costs per unit of AUM and/or increase revenues. Several important issues need to be recognized.

The low-fee section of the market has the largest economies of scale. Where are economies of scale most likely to be found for hedge funds? Scale economies are most pronounced in the administrative, compliance, and distribution functions. In addition, the relatively fixed nature of marketing expenses favors large companies. Because investment platforms can scale well up to the point of capacity, it is important to know the dynamics of firm scalability as well as the capacity of the firm's strategy or strategies. What determines how scalable the investment function really is?

Scalability of the enterprise depends on investment style (in particular, active hedge fund performance, including fees, versus passive funds and ETFs available at low cost in the market), the asset selection universe or opportunity set, asset research coverage, and the nature and availability of human capital for the enterprise. Therefore, it is not immediately clear that high-conviction management can be scaled significantly; the best managers may leave for boutique funds when a cultural conflict arises, and the corporate philosophy, environment, or investment style may change. If taken too far, increasing the scale of the enterprise can upset the sometimes fragile balance between the size of AUM and the creation of alpha.

Finally, growth through merger and acquisition can lead to operational efficiencies, on the one hand, but can harm morale and have a disruptive effect on many levels of management, on the other hand.

Positioning. How can a hedge fund management firm best position itself for growth in light of challenges posed by diminished confidence as a result of the financial crisis and the weaknesses it exposed?

The clear answer to this question is to emphasize the central importance of transparency in product descriptions, fee structures, and the investment process. The financial crisis reflected the truth that some asset management firms did not fully understand the nature of the products they were offering to clients. If the asset management firm does not understand the product, it cannot explain the product to the client. Although transparency is often promoted as an issue limited to the relationship between the client and the asset management firm, the first step to providing transparency for the client is that the asset management firm be internally transparent and understand the nature of the product it is offering to the client.

Another important response is to focus on client satisfaction as a major criterion for managers at all stages of the value chain. This criterion includes, but is by no means limited to, an emphasis on education of not only the client but also the intermediary that services the client, especially in managing unreasonable expectations. The global financial crisis was an important learning experience for everyone in the asset management industry.

A third important response is to encourage the proactive involvement of industry associations in developing industry standards for product descriptions and risk. This response is perhaps most important as it relates to the difficult relationship between the industry and its regulators.

Risk

The four key risk challenges for alternative asset management in both the short and the medium term are operational risk, market risk, regulatory risk, and legal risk.

Operational Risk. Operational risk is the most significant risk factor currently facing the alternative asset management business. Here, we use the Basel definition, that operational risk is the risk of direct or indirect loss resulting from inadequate or failed internal processes, people, or systems or from external events, excluding market or reputational risk.[13] To address this risk, the alternative asset management industry must follow state-of-the-art operational due diligence practices at every level of the organization.

First and most important, every alternative asset management firm must understand that operational due diligence is central to its business model. This understanding goes beyond merely increasing the budget allocation to due diligence. Prior to the Madoff scandal, operational due diligence was seen as a necessary cost imposed by regulators on asset management firms. Since Madoff, operational due diligence has been seen as part of the value proposition, particularly regarding delegated funds management. Where fund failures are highly predictable, not doing the necessary operational due diligence can have serious consequences indeed. Advanced IT solutions are emerging to address this need.

An often-overlooked aspect of operational due diligence is the need to periodically perform an external audit of IT infrastructure. With the growing complexity of instruments and markets, updating legacy IT platforms to adapt to this ever-changing environment is a constant challenge. The May 2010 flash crash and more recent trading outages at major exchanges showed that failures in the IT infrastructure can have widespread ramifications. Thus, external audits of the firm's IT infrastructure must be conducted to

---

[13]"The Regulatory Treatment of Operational Risk," BCBS Working Paper 8 (September 2001).

ensure that it is robust enough to meet the challenges posed by the changing market environment.

The growing complexity of the trading environment suggests a need for substantial improvements in counterparty and collateral management, specifically with respect to over-the-counter derivatives—an area of great potential for advances in information technology. Standard practice until now has been to concentrate on the immediate counterparties to each transaction. The experience of the recent financial crisis, however, has shown the importance of accounting for the systemic risk of those counterparties and the extent to which a liquidity crisis will negatively affect their ability to deliver on the terms of their contracts.[14]

The collapse of Bear Sterns, Lehman Brothers, and other major financial institutions in the United States in 2008 made clear the importance of using independent asset valuations whenever feasible. That illiquid assets are frequently "marked to model" rather than "marked to market" suggests the importance of external and independent valuations of fund assets. Such valuation is an important due diligence function, and the increase in the transparency of the valuation process may increase the confidence of both outside investors and those responsible for managing the in-house trading function.

Related to the importance of independent asset valuation is the critical role played by well-resourced and recognized external auditors. The Madoff case is the best possible example of the perils that follow from relying on the advice of small auditors. Not only do large accounting firms have access to tools and techniques unavailable to smaller accounting firms, but they also have significant reputational capital at stake and perform their own internal operational due diligence before accepting asset management firms as clients.

Moreover, the due diligence function itself needs to be rethought. The standard approach typically relies on a check-box, bottom-up analysis of reports collected at local levels. Processes, people, and systems can fail in many ways, and the sheer volume of information in due diligence reports that filter up the management chain becomes so general as to be of limited use. An operational failure involving a conflict of interest at a local or branch office may have limited impact on the asset management firm as a whole. The aggregated information may become so general, however, as to miss important operational failures at the organization's headquarters.

---

[14]An approach to this problem is to define a methodology for quantifying the extent to which each financial institution is exposed to systemic risk. See, for example, V. Acharya, C. Brownlees, R. Engle, F. Farazmand, and M. Richardson, "Measuring Systemic Risk," in *Regulating Wall Street*, edited by V. Acharya, T. Cooley, M. Richardson, and I. Walter (Hoboken, NJ: John Wiley & Sons, 2011).

Part of the problem is that the operational due diligence function is typically designed to meet the bare minimum regulatory requirements, which may not have been designed to meet challenges not thought of when the requirements were established. These minimal standards did not generally match the problems faced by a particular asset management firm. Thus, the operational due diligence was not regarded with great seriousness by many asset management firms.

The challenge facing the industry now and into the future is to restore investor confidence. The most effective way to do that is to improve operational transparency. One way to accomplish this objective is to convince investors, regulators, and other stakeholders that the alternative asset management company takes operational due diligence seriously.

Market Risk. Here, market risk is examined from the point of view of the enterprise rather than the point of view of the investor/client. For that reason, it is important to go beyond market volatility to consider extreme, or tail, events that can affect the viability of the enterprise. To address market risk, stress-test analysis must go beyond the standard VaR approach. It must reexamine the short-term incentives given to managers throughout the organization and improve transparency at all levels of the organization.

The recent financial crisis made clear the importance of advanced stress testing for worst-case scenarios. Extreme market events can cause a significant drawdown of assets under management, not merely because of the revaluation of assets but also because of investor withdrawals and private equity funds making capital calls. During the crisis, at the worst possible time for investors, investor demand for withdrawals caused many hedge funds to forbid redemptions.

Investor demand for asset drawdowns can significantly challenge the business model of alternative asset managers in two ways. The organization can face a liquidity crisis as it attempts to meet current and anticipated investor withdrawals. At the same time, revenues, determined as a fraction of AUM, suffer a substantial decline. The stress tests must accommodate both contingencies.

Standard approaches to stress testing involve VaR measures computed with either historical data or Monte Carlo approaches. These approaches can be mechanical in application and rarely consider revenue loss and liquidity demands that may challenge the viability of the management firm. Indeed, at the enterprise level, VaR can become part of the problem rather than part of the solution.

Mechanically applied VaR controls can also have the adverse consequence of providing managers with a false sense of security. For example, when no effective risk management practices are in place, a manager can be lulled into complacency by a string of persistent positive returns that precede a significant drawdown of AUM in a negative market environment. Perhaps that is why many managed funds missed the massive Madoff hedge fund fraud. Standard VaR analysis of the suspiciously persistent positive returns would have indicated that Madoff was an extremely low-risk asset manager.

In the aftermath of the global financial crisis, many observers have pointed to undue reliance on short-term incentives as a leading cause of the crisis and of the failure of many large and respected financial enterprises. Thus, many regulators have called for a reevaluation of incentive contracts in the financial sectors. The alternative asset management business is not immune to this concern. Short-term incentives can encourage allocations to assets that generate persistent short-term profits at the expense of significant tail risk for the enterprise as a whole. There is also the issue of soft-dollar accounts and the adverse short-term incentives they create for portfolio managers and others involved in asset allocation decisions.

Concern about incentives raises a more general issue related to transparency—in particular, the complexity of many of the financial products of asset management firms. Events of the 2007–08 financial crisis revealed that many managers did not understand the characteristics of the complex financial products they were selling to clients and did not appreciate the risks they were taking in the name of the firm. They either did not know or, given the focus on short-term profits and remuneration that these products generated, chose not to understand. Greater transparency is just good business practice, not only in terms of client relations but also in terms of enterprise risk management within the firm.

Regulatory Risk. Financial regulation *per se* has not been a major source of risk for the alternative asset management enterprise, which is traditionally lightly regulated. In Europe, the United States, and Asia, the regulatory environment is in a state of flux, however, which suggests greater regulation in the future. Uncertainty about future regulations is thus a significant source of risk, for its potential impact both on investor flows and on competitiveness. This concern suggests that industry associations have an important role to play in mediating the relationship between regulators and the industry and in resolving regulatory uncertainty.

This mediation role can provide information in two directions. Regulatory risk is largely a result of a lack of transparency in the rule-making process. By becoming actively involved in that process, industry associations can effectively transmit industry concerns to regulators. In return, the associations can give industry participants advance notice of prospective changes in rules and regulations that may affect the way they operate and the terms under which investors may commit funds. An important function for industry associations is to urge regulators to give advance notice to firms in the industry regarding future regulatory initiatives. There should be no surprises that would adversely affect the risk calculations and exposure of asset management entities.

The role of industry associations is not limited to that of being a conduit of information. They can take a proactive role in influencing the nature of the regulatory environment in which alternative asset management firms operate. According to a report published in the *New York Times* in March 2007, Goldman Sachs spent more money lobbying the US Congress on proposed changes in laws governing the alternative asset management business than did the entire hedge fund industry.[15] It is not surprising, then, that the hedge fund industry has had only limited influence in shaping the regulatory agenda that followed the US financial crisis. This situation now appears to be changing.

A positive relationship between the industry and the regulators can foster and promote the development of effective self-regulatory mechanisms. The development of strong and robust self-regulatory mechanisms may help offset any incentive on the part of regulators to institute mandatory requirements that may not be in the best interests of the industry or its clients.

Finally, one of the most important roles for industry associations is to advocate harmonization of regulations, certainly throughout Europe, that affect the asset management industry. Without harmonization, there is the possibility of regulatory arbitrage and a flight to the least restrictive jurisdiction, which would run precisely counter to the objective of increasing investor confidence and transparency.

Legal Risk. Legal risk is defined here as the risk that emerges when the alternative asset management firm faces liabilities in its relationship with its investors, but those liabilities are implied, not explicitly defined in the contractual obligations of the firm.

An obvious response to this risk is to strengthen the legal and compliance functions within the asset management firm. Without a strong culture of compliance, individuals and groups within the firm may create products and engage in sales and marketing activities that lead to significant costs and adverse legal obligations for the firm.

---

[15]"Wall Street's Campaign Contributions and Lobbyist Expenditures" (http://wallstreetwatch. org/reports/part2.pdf).

As with other dimensions of risk, transparency is key in legal risk management. An important way to reduce legal risk is to carefully review the terms of product offerings to clarify them and improve transparency. As noted, firms sometimes do not completely understand the characteristics of products they are offering to clients. As a result, clients may not be well informed about these characteristics and firms could be legally liable should events occur that lead to a loss in value of the products.

Costs

In the foreseeable operating environment, the business model of many alternative asset management firms is challenged by the fact that costs may rise while the revenue base does not keep pace. This possibility has focused attention on the general lack of transparency in the cost structures of the alternative asset management business. The business needs to deal with operating leverage that arises from the fact that many costs are fixed and do not scale to AUM, a prime determinant of revenue for firms. And there is the fact that costs tend to rise as a business becomes more complex and more heavily regulated.

Operating Cost. Many alternative asset management firms face a challenge in understanding and measuring their cost structure for both internal and external stakeholders. The alternative asset management business is unusual in the difficulty it faces in appropriately allocating costs among various product lines. So, firms must adopt transparent managerial accounting practices to understand and control costs along the entire value chain.

The first and most obvious point is to apply cost-accounting disciplines that are common in other industries but that have not been generally applied in the alternative asset management industry up to this point. When revenues are strong and positive for all product lines, the firms usually have no great incentive to examine costs and the pricing of various products. The financial crisis has emphasized the importance of controlling costs, however, and determining an appropriate basis for pricing products.

Because of these challenges, firms must examine and reappraise costs broken down by product, market data, and customer along the entire value chain. Product pricing must reflect the cost of providing that product, and products should be reexamined whenever the cost of providing the product exceeds the revenue that product generates.

Alternative asset management firms also need to understand the cost of serving clients. In the past, the focus has been on increasing AUM, seemingly at any cost. Too little recognition has been given to management of the client service function and to the fact that certain products require much greater customer service than others. An appropriate analysis of costs and revenues might lead to a pruning of the product offerings, with those products surviving that yield the highest revenue per unit cost.

A related point is the importance of implementing effective transfer pricing within the organization so that the products are effectively costed out. In the past, common costs associated with research (especially, IT functions) were arbitrarily assigned to product lines; sometimes, there was no cost allocation of any kind. This practice inevitably led to the result that weaker products were cross-subsidized by stronger ones.

A common cost that is extremely difficult to allocate appropriately is the hidden cost associated with maintaining embedded information systems technology. Managers often fail to recognize that this technology often has a short shelf life because of rapid changes in the trading environment. Often, maintaining otherwise obsolete technology is more costly than investing in new technology. Because the necessary maintenance expenditures are not calibrated appropriately, however, managers may maintain the old systems rather than invest in new systems. They need to understand the magnitude of these costs and how they affect processes they use and the product mix they offer.

Finally, the cost issue is compounded in the case of funds of hedge funds, which promise expertise in the selection of hedge fund managers, access to hedge funds that are otherwise difficult to access, and some degree of diversification. In return, investments in funds of funds involve fees on fees—noted earlier as 1.5% on top of hedge fund fees of 2% plus 20% of gains. The 3.5% fixed fees payable with 100% probability create a high performance hurdle in a volatile and low-growth environment. Nevertheless, the fund-of-funds industry grew rapidly during the early 2000s, with global assets of US$593 billion in 2008 (compared with US$1.4 trillion for all hedge funds). One of the consequences of the global financial crisis was the revelation that due diligence of funds of funds was less rigorous than assumed—many of the investments in the Madoff Ponzi scheme were generated by funds of funds—nor did they provide much protection against the subsequent market collapse. Since that time, the proportionate role of funds of funds has declined significantly

Operating Leverage. Operating leverage arises because the alternative asset management business is typically characterized by high fixed costs set against a highly variable revenue base. On the one hand, because most AUM fee structures imply that revenues are tied to AUM, significant economies of scale seem possible in the provision of asset management services. On the other hand, a market downturn that leads to a swift reduction in AUM, through both capital losses and investor withdrawals, can challenge the business model of the asset management industry. To examine this question in any depth, it is necessary to study with some care both the cost structures and the extent to which revenue does, indeed, depend on the scale of operations.

Because the benefits of operating leverage are given by economies of scale in the provision of asset management services, techniques must be used that accurately measure how large these economies might be and how big the firm must be to build on the resulting cost advantage. These answers depend, in turn, on an accurate assessment of the cost structure associated with each product and how scalable the investment function actually is. In many cases, capacity constraints limit the potential gains from economies of scale.

If AUM and their associated revenues fall below the fixed costs of performing back-office functions in-house, one can at least consider outsourcing them. Outsourcing does allow otherwise fixed costs to be scaled to the size of the enterprise. There is a critical scale, however, at which it makes sense to bring these functions back in-house.

In the past, the interests of hedge funds and other alternative asset managers were generally assumed to be best served by increasing AUM regardless of how much it cost to service those assets. In the past 5–10 years, however, the focus of the enterprise has shifted from maximizing the size of AUM to a consideration of what offerings are more or less profitable. This approach leads to conversations with clients about what fee structures are most appropriate.

An important new development is the recognition that new and sophisticated products that are now coming to market imply higher personnel costs in terms of new hires or training of existing staff. These costs should be applied against the new products being offered instead of being added to the general administrative costs overhead. At the same time, they simply add to the fixed costs of the enterprise unless the new products represent a net increase in AUM.

But costs associated with many of these new products are not fixed costs; they vary with AUM. Examples include the relatively new "quant" products that rely extensively on the use of market data and information feeds (for example, index licensing fees). These costs are frequently scalable because they are typically charged as a percentage of AUM.

An approach to the operating leverage problem, in the context of institutional business, is to consider alternative product delivery vehicles, such as managed accounts. The problem of operating leverage arises because, in the majority of cases, fees are locked into an AUM structure whereas costs are relatively fixed. Reexamining fee structures is difficult and/or costly at this time, although some clients are likely to push the industry down this path. The asset management company also needs to question the legal and regulatory costs associated with alternative product delivery vehicles, costs that offset the potential advantages of alternative revenue structures.

Trading Costs. Trading costs have generally risen since the financial crisis; trading and liquidity have been slow to return to precrisis levels and, in some areas of the bond markets, have remained problematic—especially because the major market makers have withdrawn from proprietary trading. These costs extend beyond commissions and market impact to include the costs associated with the IT necessary to adapt to the emerging trading environment. This cost challenge can best be addressed by adapting the trading function within the asset management firm to the new trading environment.

The first and necessary step toward accomplishing this goal is to reduce trading costs by lessening the reliance on legacy IT infrastructures to handle the evolving trading environment. Too often, the solution is to merely adapt existing IT platforms to the new trading patterns. This approach is costly and inefficient and may be ineffective. Rather than simply throwing money into old technology, a better idea is to develop new IT infrastructure to deal with the changing technological environment.

A second approach is to consider alternative trading strategies, such as algorithmic trading, and methods and platforms that can reduce commissions and market-impact charges. A good example is high-conviction managers circumventing capacity limitations by using dark pools and other trading technologies. A related approach is to develop and implement STP functions across the entire value chain.

An important step is to unbundle research and transaction services. By eliminating soft-dollar accounts and separately outsourcing the research and investment services functions, firms can not only control trading costs but also appropriately cost out and attribute the service function costs to each product area. In addition, the existence of soft-dollar accounts creates an adverse incentive to trade when trading is not strictly necessary.

Asset management firms are becoming global operators with trading functions around the world. An important element of cost control is to professionalize the trading functions throughout developed and developing markets. The internationalization of asset management firms presents an opportunity to introduce best practice techniques across the enterprise rather than to delegate monitoring and control to each regional unit.

In summary, although trading costs have risen because of changes in the trading function since the financial crisis, alternative asset management firms can take advantage of the new opportunities to reduce trading costs significantly by adapting to these new circumstances.

Regulatory Compliance Costs. In response to the financial crisis, regulatory compliance costs have increased—in some cases, substantially. These costs are unavoidable and are a necessary cost of doing business. The industry has an opportunity to treat regulatory compliance in a positive and constructive way that will restore investor confidence in the industry and encourage transparency. To achieve this objective, regulatory compliance must be framed to provide a long-term, confidence-building exercise for each company's clients and stakeholders.

An unintended consequence of the more strictly enforced compliance regime for hedge funds is that it provides an opening for industry associations to impress upon regulators the urgent need to harmonize investment company regulations across national borders. This move would reduce or eliminate regulatory arbitrage and create a level playing field for all. In addition, the existence of a uniform international regulatory regime can only help increase the investor confidence that was so badly shaken by the financial crisis and the Madoff fraud, which crossed international borders and exploited differences in regulatory regimes.

Alternatives beyond Hedge Funds

Although hedge funds are the largest category of managed assets defined as alternatives, leveraged buyout funds, venture capital funds, and others that specialize in such asset classes as timber, arable farmland, and natural resources have developed over the years. Most of these funds fall under the umbrella category of "private equity," although private debt, commodity futures, and other types of funds are to be found in the alternative asset universe. The objective, as always, is to achieve superior returns relative to benchmarks and/or low correlations. Microfinance and venture capital funds provide some examples.

A recent study found that pools of loans by microfinance institutions (MFIs) show no statistically significant relationship with global market movements.[16] Comparing the market risk of the leading MFIs with that of the leading emerging-market financial institutions, the study found that MFIs show significantly less sensitivity to global capital markets in terms of income and assets. When the global market risk of MFIs is compared with that of emerging-market commercial banks, MFIs consistently show low correlations for key performance parameters.

To a significant degree, MFIs thus seem detached from global capital markets, but they do not seem nearly as detached from their domestic

---

[16]Nicolas Krauss and Ingo Walter, "Can Microfinance Reduce Portfolio Volatility?" *Economic Development and Cultural Change*, vol. 58 (October 2009).

markets. Still, overall domestic risk exposure might be lower than for most alternative emerging-market investments. The results suggest that MFIs may have useful diversification value for international portfolio investors wishing to diversify away their country risk.

For emerging-market domestic investors—who may have a much more limited capacity to diversify—domestic microfinance investments do not seem to provide significant portfolio diversification advantages. The difference in market risk between microfinance and other emerging-market institutions is based on a generally nonpublic ownership structure that reduces dependence on capital markets, lowers the international exposure of microfinance clients, and lowers operational and financial leverage. It follows that, as the microfinance industry matures, market risk associated with MFIs will increase—although, because of client characteristics, most likely to a lower level than for most other emerging-market investments.

Over time, one would expect emerging markets as an asset class to be subject to "correlation creep" as a result of higher levels of financial integration, which brings significant economic benefits but also reduces the value of the asset class for diversification purposes. This scenario, however, may not be true under market stress, as in the 2013 US Federal Reserve quantitative easing "tapering" announcement, which disproportionately affected emerging markets as an asset class. Hence, the search continues for alternative asset classes and subclasses, such as "frontier" markets and securitized microfinance loans.

Leveraged buyout funds—a type of private equity fund—are another example of alternative pooled assets, albeit with a structure that is not broadly available to most investors. The objective is to raise funds from qualified investors (mainly institutional investors and wealthy individuals) and acquire underperforming firms with a view to restructuring them and then exiting via a trade sale or a public offering. Besides making strategic and operating improvements, buyout fund managers—who usually invest alongside outside investors and reap a large share of the gains—often add large amounts of debt to the capital structure of targeted firms to turbocharge the return on equity in successful deals.

Despite different investment goals and underlying assets, the dynamics of buyout firms and venture capital firms—the other major type of private equity firm—are not dissimilar. Such firms as Blackstone, TCI, Bain Capital, and KKR have long histories in the private equity business, which has migrated from being US-centric to being essentially global.

The economic contribution of private equity firms has long been controversial. On the positive side is elimination of agency problems that typically exist in listed corporations where the interests of managers and shareholders are misaligned. The pressures created by the actions of the private equity firm thus result in better management performance—as well as detachment from the regulatory environment of public companies and the pressure for short-term share price gains. On the negative side are allegations of industrial dismemberment, profiteering, and excessive use of leverage that add risk and can detract from economic growth and sustainability. One argument suggests that leveraging an index such as the S&P 500 to the extent that private equity firms leverage the firms they control would produce more or less the same returns; if that is the case, the other arguments used to defend the industry have little substance.

Given the use of leverage, the private equity industry is highly sensitive to financial market conditions. The industry ramped up investable funds globally during the financial boom of 2003–2007 but then collapsed spectacularly during the financial crisis and the recession that followed in 2008–2011. Improved stock market performance in 2012–2015 reinvigorated the industry in terms of both new inflows of investable funds seeking yield in an ultra-low-interest-rate environment and investment opportunities associated with the economic wreckage of the recession and the ensuing sluggish economic recovery.

6. Private Wealth Management

Global individual wealth can take a variety of forms, encompassing financial assets (currency, bank balances, stocks, bonds, etc.) and real assets (commodities, precious stones, *objets d'art*, real estate, and other asset classes that have some sort of actual or potential market value). These assets range across the entire liquidity, risk, and return spectrum, from cash to real estate to private equity investments. The ability to measure wealth at any time depends on the existence of a market for each asset (hence, the importance of liquidity) and the ability to mark to market. Because wealthy individuals' assets are often held in illiquid form, global wealth estimates tend to be somewhat inaccurate. A variety of intermediaries are engaged in wealth management, including trust companies, major banks and financial conglomerates, investment banks, private banks and boutiques, individual financial advisers, and family and multifamily offices. Market shares are highly fragmented, and wealthy investors have plenty of choice.

Global Distribution of Wealth

The investable wealth of high-net-worth households was estimated at roughly US$164 trillion at the end of 2014.[17] This figure includes all asset classes (except real assets) held by the 29 million individuals and households with a net worth exceeding US$1 million (representing about 0.6% of the adult world population), which suggests a heavy concentration of wealth globally. **Figure 9** shows the degree of global wealth concentration; **Table 8** shows the residencies of the upper end of the wealth pyramid for 2014; and **Table 9** shows levels and changes in aggregate wealth to be managed. These data suggest substantial heterogeneity in terms of wealth levels and thus asset management requirements.

Tables 8 and 9 show that, like private wealth itself, the geographical dispersion of wealthy households has substantial skewness. The OECD countries—especially the United States—are heavily overrepresented relative to population. This picture seems to be changing, however, with disproportionate wealth growth in Asia Pacific relative to North America and Europe. This trend can be explained in terms of both newly created wealth and the performance of existing portfolios. The factors that determine where wealth is distributed by source and region (held both onshore and offshore) around the world are per capita income, wealth distribution, and government policies.

---

[17]Boston Consulting Group, *Global Wealth 2015: Winning the Growth Game* (Boston: BCG, 2015).

Figure 9.   Global Wealth Pyramids, 2014

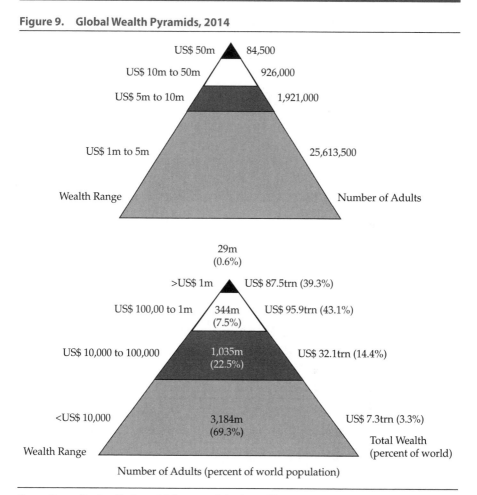

Source: James Davies, Rodrigo Lluberas, and Anthony Shorrocks, "The Global Wealth Databook 2015," Credit Suisse (2015).

Per Capita Income. Wealth is a "stock" measure, and income is a "flow" measure. Macroeconomic outcomes greatly affect wealth levels, as evidenced by a decade of economic growth in the United States during the 1990s and early 2000s versus a period of stagnation in Japan and by the periodic booms and busts seen in some of the emerging-market countries. Higher-income countries and regions naturally tend to harbor larger stores of wealth than do lower-income ones.

Wealth Distribution. Endowments of capital ownership and property rights, as well as education levels and other sources of earning power, differ

Table 8. Dollar Millionaires by Location of Residence

Location	Percentage
United States	39%
Japan	13
France	8
United Kingdom	6
Germany	5
Italy	4
China	3
Australia	3
Canada	3
Switzerland	2
Sweden	1
Spain	1
Netherlands	1
Rest of the world	11

Source: Credit Suisse, Global Private Banking Database (2015).

Table 9. Private Financial Wealth: Location and Growth, 2012–2014

Area	Wealth (US$ trillions)				Average Annual Change		
	2012	2013	2014	2019E	2012–2013	2013–2014	2014–2019E
North America	42.2	48.2	50.8	62.5	14.2%	5.6%	4.2%
Western Europe	36.3	37.2	39.6	49.0	2.4	6.6	4.3
Eastern Europe	2.1	2.4	2.9	4.6	14.6	18.8	10.0
Japan	13.5	14.0	14.3	15.5	3.3	2.5	1.6
Latin America	3.2	3.4	3.7	6.6	5.9	10.5	12.0
Middle East and Africa	4.6	5.2	5.7	8.8	11.5	9.4	9.3
Asia Pacific (ex Japan)	28.8	36.5	47.3	75.1	27.0	29.4	9.7
Global	130.7	146.8	164.3	222.1	12.3	11.9	6.2

Notes: Private wealth was measured across all private households. All growth rates are nominal. With the exception of Argentina, numbers for all years were converted to US dollars at average 2014 exchange rates to exclude the effect of currency fluctuations. Percentage changes and global total of private financial wealth are based on complete (not rounded) numbers. Calculations for all years shown are based on the same methodology. E = estimated.

Source: Boston Consulting Group, *Global Wealth 2015.*

significantly among countries and regions. Market processes may generate wide differences in the distribution of wealth among countries around the world, even when economic size and per capita income are comparable.

Government Policies. The treatment by governments of accumulation of wealth tends to result from a confluence of historical, cultural, and sociological factors that generate a political concept of a "fair" distribution. Some societies have always regarded wealth as evidence of exploitation and economic parasitism. This political overlay drives national policy with respect to taxation, expropriation, and other policy measures affecting the wealthy and is often based on the politics of envy. Policy changes affecting wealth can be gradual or abrupt, and those who have assets to conserve tend to be highly sensitive to such changes.

Taken together, these three factors probably explain much of the geographical global distribution of wealth—not only where wealth can be found but also where it is individually held rather than institutionalized. There are plenty of "rich" societies where seriously wealthy individuals are few and far between—or have taken up residence elsewhere—while other societies have seriously wealthy residents in abundance. If wealth accumulation is heavily taxed or heavily institutionalized (e.g., in the form of pension funds or assets controlled by the state, labor unions, or cooperatives), societies have little interest in private banking. Wealthy individuals and families tend to emerge where markets have been allowed to determine individual income and wealth levels, and it is in these locations where private banking services are of greatest interest.

Sources of Personal Wealth

Wealth is usually the product of past or present income from the provision of goods or services, together with returns (interest, dividends, capital gains) earned on the accumulated assets over time. Thus, wealth can normally be considered evidence of significant economic contributions in a market-oriented system. When wealth is inherited, it reflects an ancestor's contribution.

But wealth can also be amassed *at the expense of* the rest of society through the unchecked exercise of monopoly power, extortion, racketeering, corruption, insider trading, drug trafficking, tax evasion (as opposed to tax avoidance), and so on. Nobody likes to talk about such things, but they do exist. Wealth is wealth. Classifying wealth in terms of its origins can provide a useful basis for the assessment of client attitudes, market segmentation, and private banking requirements.

- *Family (inherited) wealth* involves the transfer of assets from one generation to another. This form of wealth tends to be sensitive to redistribution-oriented national fiscal and economic policies, especially estate taxation. It can arise from any of the other sources of wealth listed here. Heavy concentrations of family wealth are traditionally found in Western Europe (the home of "classic" private banking), North America, and parts of Asia.

- *Corporate wealth* is typically generated through service as a management employee of a corporation in the form of salaries, bonuses, deferred compensation, stock option plans, and severance payments. The greatest concentration of this form of wealth is found in the United States because US levels of executive compensation (usually through stock option grants) are higher than anywhere else in the world.

- *Entrepreneurial wealth* tends to be accumulated over the lifetime of an individual who is either sole owner or co-owner of a business enterprise. The key word is *owner*, not *employee*. Entrepreneurial wealth may remain "paper" (illiquid) wealth for extended periods and be realized only when the enterprise is sold or goes public. Concentrations of such wealth are traditionally found in Europe and Asia (often in family-owned and family-controlled businesses). Entrepreneurial wealth is also found in the United States. Massive new wealth concentrations resulted from startups in such leading-edge economic sectors as technology and biotech—especially in the boom periods of the late 1990s—as well as hedge funds and private equity firms.

- *Political wealth* may represent "gifts" from constituents or the proceeds of corruption in political office at various levels within national or regional governments, as well as private businesses benefiting from official corruption. Sources include misappropriation of public funds, bribery, extortion, political contributions, kickbacks, and financial holdings linked to government contracts. Public servants are rarely highly compensated, but some wealthy former public servants did not start out that way. The incentives underlying ill-gotten gains are ubiquitous. They are typically leveraged into serious wealth in environments that have poorly developed markets and that lack transparent, rule-based democratic politics, legal systems, and administrative infrastructures. Political wealth has thus tended to arise disproportionately in some of the emerging-market and transitional economies of Africa, Asia, and Eastern Europe.

- *Criminal wealth* comprises assets traced to organized crime, extortion, theft of public and private property, financial fraud, arms trafficking, the drug trade, and other illegal activities, usually laundered into standard asset classes and invested in various ways. Criminal activities exist in all parts of the world, but such activities probably give rise to more wealth where there are less open and less transparent markets, combined with poor law enforcement.

Private wealth management targets the first three of these sources of wealth, which probably represent some 85% to 90% of total private assets under management. The last two categories present unique problems. Contamination of a private asset management franchise as a result of a major corruption or criminal investigation (including tax evasion and money laundering) can seriously injure a firm's reputation or, at the least, require a great deal of explaining to clients. No one who values reputation and privacy enjoys being a client of an asset manager who is undergoing intense scrutiny in a criminal investigation. Knowing what clients to avoid can be just as important as knowing what clients to attract.

Private Client Asset Management Objectives

Like other investors, wealthy investors base asset allocation choices on their relative preferences for risk and return. The market value of a portfolio of assets is driven by the risk–return attributes of the various assets contained in the portfolio—where the risk associated with an individual asset is based on the variance of its expected future returns. The risk embedded in an entire asset portfolio, in turn, is a product of correlations between the returns of all the assets contained in it as well as of the individual asset risks. Consequently, there is value in diversification across individual assets, asset classes, political-economic environments, and other "buckets" (asset allocation categories) that are believed to be less than perfectly correlated. The lower the correlations between asset buckets, the greater the power of diversification.

Wealthy people are explicitly or implicitly looking for "efficient" portfolios that minimize risk for a given target rate of return or that maximize total returns for a given level of portfolio risk. Wealthy people differ from nonwealthy people in that they have a lot to preserve, so they tend to use relatively conservative asset allocation approaches. They are also sensitive to confidentiality, trust, and service quality.

Defined in such general terms, wealth is a purely economic measure. It does not necessarily equate to an individual's own assessment of his or her personal worth in a broader context, which is affected by many other factors.

Wealthy people differ in the satisfaction they derive from an increase in their level of wealth and how that wealth may affect family members and other eventual beneficiaries. They are influenced by prevailing social, political, religious, and philosophical attitudes toward wealth and the satisfaction derived from charitable giving. And they differ in the time and resources they want to spend on wealth management.

This complex of issues, which tends to color their vision of the true value of what they have, must be intuitively understood by the private banker. Achieving this understanding is not easy and is usually personal in nature. Successful private bankers thus require a unique combination of skills in offering a broad value chain of services and advice.

The objectives of private clients tend to be more idiosyncratic than those of many other financial services segments, such as mass-market retail and business customers. The objectives reflect an amalgam of needs, among which capital preservation and yield, tax efficiency, confidentiality, and service level are critical.

- *Capital preservation vs. total return.* As noted, traditional private banking clients tend to focus on wealth preservation because of uncertain political and economic conditions, changeable government policies, and fickle markets. They demand the utmost in discretion from private bankers, with whom they often maintain lifelong relationships initiated by personal contacts. Such traditional clients continue to be important but have gradually yielded to a more active and sophisticated group: clients who are increasingly aware of the opportunity costs of poor investment performance and who often focus on total returns calibrated against benchmarks. They may prefer that gains accrue as capital appreciation rather than as interest or dividend income, and they often demand a much more active investment approach in which they themselves want to be involved.

- *Security.* At the end of the 20th century, the world was arguably more stable than ever before. The probability of revolution, war, and gross confiscatory taxation had declined just about everywhere. Still, many wealthy clients remained highly security conscious and were thus prepared to trade yield for stability and safety. The 2001 terrorist attacks in the United States and turmoil in the Middle East, West Asia, and parts of Latin America—together with the financial crisis of 2007–2008—seemed to justify such concerns. With turmoil in the Middle East, Eastern Europe, Africa, and parts of Asia, the insecurity has been amplified in the current decade.

- *Tax efficiency.* Many private clients are exposed to high average or marginal tax rates. Nobody likes to pay taxes, but the wealthy are under more pressure than anyone else; in the United States, for example, the highest-income 5% of taxpayers are estimated to generate well over half the country's income tax revenue. Where fiscal burdens can be legally avoided under the tax code, such tax avoidance is a valuable service to the private client. And in some environments, the same is true of tax evasion, which occurs in violation of the applicable tax code and which financial institutions in a number of countries facilitate. Politicians like to target "the rich" but are often surprised at how little of ambitious public spending programs can actually be financed in this way.

- *Discretion.* Confidentiality is a key attribute of private banking. It means keeping sensitive information away from others because disclosure can cause damage to the individual concerned. One might expect the rich to have more reasons than others to keep secrets. So, the watchword of the private banking profession is "discretion, discretion, discretion."

- *Service level.* Personal services provided to private banking clients can be exceptional and are considered critical in cementing relationships and client loyalty to a particular financial institution. Extraordinary personal services may save time, reduce anxiety, increase efficiency, and make the whole wealth management process convenient and pleasant. Such services allow banks to use particular ways to show their commitment to, and understanding of, clients who are accustomed to a high level of personal service in their daily lives.

Perhaps more than in other parts of the financial services industry, the essence of private banking is to accurately identify each client's unique characteristics and goals and apply the necessary flexibility and expertise to satisfy them in a highly competitive marketplace.

For financial institutions, the private banking client base offers a number of attractions. In terms of competitive dynamics, it has substantial growth potential because of the increasing demographic importance of the wealthy in the main industrialized and developing countries. Notwithstanding the rapid rise in the number of firms targeting this market segment, it is still generally considered to have attractive business potential. "Asset gathering" among high-net-worth and ultra-high-net-worth individuals has become the objective, and private client services have become a key part of the strategy.

The range of private client services is broad and must be executed seamlessly. The essential factor is to offer a truly personal service that focuses on the asset side and sometimes on the liability side of the client's balance sheet.

　　　81

Moreover, because of the highly personal nature of private banking, clients generally prefer to "stay with" a particular firm if possible, which decreases sensitivity to price and performance, facilitates product cross-selling, and enables institutions to compete on qualitative variables instead of pricing alone. The business is "capital light," with favorable cost-to-income ratios, and capable of realizing significant economies of scale in transaction-processing and portfolio management activities.

Onshore (or, domestic) wealth management consists of the previously mentioned value chain of financial and advisory services provided within the country of residence of the wealthy client. A key difference among competing financial institutions is the wealth cutoff point for private banking clients. One bank may require a minimum of US$5 million placed in investment management accounts. Another may be more flexible—a minimum requirement of US$1 million in AUM, for example, or an even lower amount with the understanding that the client is likely to make significant additional investments. Or the minimum may be waived for the "right" client. Alternatively, a bank may require that each private banking client generate a certain amount of annual fees.

The bundling of private wealth management services makes it difficult to evaluate the value–cost relationship of each component, which potentially allows the bank to extract higher fees. And the client is likely to be less price sensitive with respect to the purchase of bundled services than with respect to the purchase of each service separately.

Although other areas of banking have been subject to a general unbundling of services as a result of a proliferation of new financial products and techniques, private banking remains an area where bundling may retain value for some time to come. And because of the existence of economies of scope, a bank can often provide several services more economically than it can provide a single service—an important rationale for the cross-selling of bank products. Because the fiduciary nature of the private wealth management relationship gives the bank access to a rich vein of client-specific information, it may retain an advantage in serving the private client that competitors find difficult to overcome.

Offshore Wealth Management

Offshore wealth management is the management in one country/region of assets owned by the citizen or resident of another country/region. It is concentrated in such major financial centers as London, Luxembourg, New York City, Hong Kong, Switzerland, and Singapore—as well as in such traditional "havens" as Antigua and Barbuda, Anguilla, Barbados, the British Virgin Islands, the Cayman Islands, Dominica, Grenada, Guernsey, the Isle of

Man, Jersey, Montserrat, Liechtenstein, the Netherlands Antilles, St. Kitts and Nevis, St. Lucia, St. Vincent, the Grenadines, Turks and Caicos, and Vanuatu, among others. **Table 10** shows the sources of wealth held offshore and the offshore locations where that wealth is held.

People want assets held outside their countries of residence for various reasons, including portfolio diversification, risks pervading the home environment, tax evasion and avoidance, escape from domestic legal and enforcement actions, and confidentiality. The core client base for offshore private banking demands both security and confidentiality. The wealthy individuals and families wish to hold funds in an offshore tax-friendly environment and in a form that will maintain its value but be protected from exposure and disclosure.

Table 10. Sources and Locations of Offshore Wealth, March 2012

Location	Amount (US$ trillion)
Origins of offshore wealth	
Western Europe	2.7
Asia Pacific[a]	2.1
Middle East and Africa	1.6
Latin America	1.0
North America	0.8
Eastern Europe	0.3
Destinations of offshore wealth	
Switzerland	2.2
Hong Kong and Singapore	1.2
Channel Islands and Dublin	1.1
Caribbean and Panama	1.1
United Kingdom	0.9
United States	0.7
Other[b]	0.7
Luxembourg	0.6

Notes: Offshore wealth is defined as assets booked in a location where the investor has no legal residence or tax domicile. Offshore estimated AUM is US$8.5 trillion.

[a]Including Japan.
[b]Includes Dubai and Monaco.

Source: Boston Consulting Group.

Financial Confidentiality[18]

Financial confidentiality—nondisclosure of financial information concerning individuals, firms, financial institutions, and governments—is an integral part of the market for all banking and financial services, fiduciary relationships, and regulatory structures. It also constitutes a "product" that has intrinsic value and can be bought and sold separately or in conjunction with other financial services.

The Demand for Financial Confidentiality. The demand for financial confidentiality can be defined as the willingness to pay for assured nondisclosure of financial information.

- *Personal financial confidentiality* usually remains in substantial compliance with applicable laws and regulations and has been well served in many countries by long-standing traditions of banking confidentiality. Indeed, financial privacy is often regarded as a cornerstone of individual liberty.

- *Business financial confidentiality* involves withholding financial information from competitors, suppliers, employees, creditors, and customers. Release of such information is undertaken only in a tightly controlled manner and, where possible, in a way that benefits the enterprise. Financial information is proprietary. It is capitalized in the value of a business to its shareholders.

- *Tax evasion* (as distinct from *tax avoidance*) is a classic source of demand for financial confidentiality. Some people are exposed to high levels of income taxation. Others are hit by confiscatory wealth taxes or death taxes. Still others feel forced by high indirect taxes or quasi taxes to escape into the underground economy. And there are those for whom the only "fair" tax is zero. Tax evasion is, by definition, illegal and passes the burden of public finance onto others. Those practicing it will be pursued under applicable civil and criminal law. It also requires varying degrees of financial confidentiality.

- *Capital flight* normally refers to the response by asset owners to an unfavorable change in the risk–return profile associated with a portfolio of assets held in a particular country, as compared with a portfolio held in other national jurisdictions. It usually involves significant conflict between the objectives of asset holders and those of their governments. It may or may not violate the law. It is always considered by the authorities to be undesirable.

---

[18]Parts of this section and the following section draw from the work I authored for "Use and Misuse of Financial Secrecy in Global Banking" in *Socially Responsible Finance and Investing: Financial Institutions, Corporations, Investors, and Activists*, edited by H.K. Baker and J.R. Nofsinger (Hoboken, NJ: John Wiley & Sons, Inc., 2012).

- *Criminals,* such as drug traffickers, not only accumulate large amounts of cash but also regularly deal in a variety of financial instruments and foreign currencies. All require ways to launder funds and eliminate paper trails that can be taken as evidence of criminal activity: Their money needs to disappear and stay that way. Bribery and corruption require no less financial confidentiality.

No matter what the motivation, the value of confidentiality depends on what may happen if disclosure occurs and on the probability of its happening. Damage can range from familial conflict and social ostracism to confiscation of assets, incremental taxes, fines, and imprisonment. Avoidance of damage is what the confidentiality seeker is after. Because damage is usually a matter of probabilities, the individual's attitude toward the risk of exposure is a critical factor in how this benefit is valued.

The Supply of Financial Confidentiality. As with the demand for confidentiality, the supply of confidentiality-oriented financial services encompasses a complex patchwork of intermediaries, conduits, and assets that provide varying degrees of safety from unwanted disclosure. Supply sources can be classified into onshore financial assets, offshore financial assets, and physical assets held either onshore or offshore.

Traditional banking practice in most countries provides for adequate confidentiality with respect to unauthorized inquiries and offers reasonable shielding of "personal" and "business" needs for privacy. Once the law gets involved, however—in civil, tax, or criminal matters—much of this protection is lost. Under applicable legal procedures, the state can also force disclosure in the event of divorce proceedings, creditor suits, inheritance matters, and tax cases—not to mention criminal actions.

Assets held abroad may offer a good deal more confidentiality because national sovereignty stops at the border and extraterritorial investigations normally require disclosure terms that are carefully and often reciprocally negotiated between governments. Bank deposits or assets in fiduciary accounts may be held abroad in jurisdictions that safeguard confidentiality through credible nondisclosure laws and blocking statutes; such jurisdictions often are also tax friendly for nonresidents. Bearer certificates, beneficial ownership structures, and shell companies may provide added protection and increase the complexity of any future paper chase.

All suppliers of financial confidentiality—whether individuals, financial institutions, or countries—have an important stake in doing their best to limit disclosure to avoid damaging the value of what they have to sell. A broad array of offshore confidentiality-oriented services and vendors thus exists—all competing with one another. Some traditional sources of confidentiality are easily available in some places but less so elsewhere. Others have been built up over generations as secure repositories and can command high premiums. A few offer confidentiality services that have no good substitutes, so fees and other costs may be quite high.

Arguably, higher levels of confidentiality involve successively greater degrees of monopolistic power in the competitive structure and organization of the market for financial confidentiality. Note the disproportionate market share of Switzerland, which has traditionally combined financial confidentiality with political and economic stability, a strong currency, and an outstanding level of private banking service.

Market Dynamics. Together with conventional motivations related to risk and return, investor behavior may also be driven by confidentiality regarding the nature, location, and composition of financial or other assets that compose a portfolio. If confidentiality is not a free good, it must be "purchased" by putting together a portfolio of assets (or a single asset class) that yields the desired level of nondisclosure. One "cost" of confidentiality to the asset holder is thus the difference between the expected yield on a confidentiality-oriented portfolio and the yield on a "benchmark portfolio" put together for the same individual if confidentiality were not a consideration.

Part of the total return differential attributable to the need for confidentiality simply reflects charges levied by financial intermediaries. Banking fees may be higher for asset holders driven by the need for confidentiality. Transactions may have to be routed in clandestine ways—through narrow markets with wider spreads or via inefficient payment conduits—which adds to transaction costs. Foreign exchange transactions, perhaps repeated several times or involving parallel (black) markets, may add further costs. Third parties, beneficial owners, lawyers, and shell companies may have to be used to enhance confidentiality—all of which involve costs.

Besides the confidentiality-related differential in the expected total return on assets, there is also the matter of differential risk. Portfolios of assets containing greater degrees of financial confidentiality are likely to be more risky. For example, assets may have to be held directly or indirectly in offshore jurisdictions, resulting in increased foreign exchange risk or country risk. Or the portfolio may be forced into a configuration that is susceptible to increased interest rate risk, and various ways of diversifying or hedging risk may be unavailable to portfolios that incorporate a high degree of confidentiality.

Agency Problems. Agency problems can vex those with substantial needs for confidentiality. An "agency" relationship exists whenever an asset owner delegates decision-making authority to the nonowning manager of a portfolio. Interpretation of investor objectives is sometimes not easy under the best of circumstances. Investor objectives may change, and the fiduciary may be uninformed or poorly advised.

The investor, in addition, may psychologically reposition his or her objectives after the fact if the portfolio has underperformed in some way and assign undeserved blame to the asset manager. Similarly, serious agency problems arise if, for example, the asset manager abuses his or her mandate by "churning" the portfolio to bolster commission income or by "stuffing" the portfolio with questionable assets. Usually, well-defined contracts between principals and agents, together with redress incorporated into banking and securities laws, provide adequate incentives for agents to make decisions that are in the interests of asset holders.

Financial confidentiality raises some unique agency issues. If confidentiality is added to the fiduciary's mandate, the job becomes much more complex. Violation of the fiduciary's role, at least in the eyes of the client, includes violation of the confidentiality mandate—even if the mandate itself is in violation of applicable laws or regulations. Ordinarily, disputes between clients and their asset managers can be taken into court in civil suits or other means of dispute resolution. But how can the asset holder take the agent to court when a foreign legal jurisdiction is involved, when it is unclear which jurisdiction governs, or when any such action would itself compromise the confidentiality that is being sought? So, the agent acquires certain immunity from the kind of redress usually available to asset holders who might be confronted by agent misconduct.

The question is whether such quasi immunity influences the behavior of the fiduciary to the detriment of the asset holder. Perhaps those seeking high levels of confidentiality are prepared to pay some agency costs so long as there are no large unaccountable losses. Perhaps competition in the asset management business, as well as traditions of prudence and competence, tends to impose constraints on abusive behavior. Still, this problem puts a real premium on selection of the offshore private banker, who must be depended on to carry out fiduciary responsibilities with great care and sensitivity to client desires without succumbing to the temptations that arise from his or her potential leverage as a "secret agent."

Interactions. Supply and demand interact in the (predominantly offshore) market for financial confidentiality, just as they do in any other market. A hierarchy of differentiated products exists, each with its own characteristics. The greater the demand, the higher the price. The more intense the competition among vendors and the easier the substitutability of confidentiality products, the lower the price.

The rational offshore client will presumably shop around, insofar as his or her position is not thereby jeopardized, to acquire an optimal mix of products at a cost (including agency costs) that makes the whole exercise worthwhile. The acquisition of offshore assets in the presence of confidentiality can thus be thought of as a rational process—one that balances a number of costs against benefits and in which the confidentiality factor is likely to alter behavior in rather predictable ways. And if confidentiality-seeking asset holders are risk averse, they may prefer rather conservative portfolios because they are seriously exposed to risk in other ways.

Regulatory and Tax Pressures on Offshore Wealth Management

Indications are that the value of financial confidentiality has been in a gradual decline as a competitive driver in the global management of private wealth. This decline is based on changing attitudes toward financial secrecy and the kinds of pressure that national tax and criminal authorities can bring to bear on foreign jurisdictions. The decline became much more serious in recent years as governments' needs for tax revenues to support social programs rose significantly and as the 2007–08 financial crisis and the accompanying bailouts of banks and other firms created major fiscal problems for virtually all countries. Together with a crackdown on money laundering, governments were clearly getting serious about putting heavy pressure on sellers of financial confidentiality, whether countries or institutions.

The focus is usually on (1) tax coordination, cooperation, and alignment among countries of residence of offshore clients; (2) tighter notification and reporting requirements imposed on banks dealing with suspect or underregulated banks and countries; (3) international agreements to expand account investigations related to money laundering, including a more intense focus on accountants and lawyers; and (4) the use of economic and political pressure in the case of noncooperating institutions and countries, including banning them from major financial markets and from doing business with financial services firms engaged in private wealth management.

In 2008, the OECD issued a set of guidelines that defined tax havens, set the outlines of cooperation with countries trying to enforce their tax statutes, and imposed sanctions on tax havens identified as "uncooperative." The OECD was concerned that laws be applied openly and consistently and that information needed by foreign tax authorities to determine a taxpayer's situation be available. Lack of transparency in one country can make it difficult, if not impossible, for tax authorities elsewhere to apply their laws effectively. Criteria include "secret rulings," negotiated tax rates, limited regulatory supervision, and a government's lack of legal access to financial records. A key feature of the OECD guidelines for identifying tax havens is to combat the persistent lack of information exchange whereby governments can obtain the knowledge needed to identify tax evaders.

To put pressure on tax haven countries, the OECD in 2008 issued a "blacklist" of nations that were not in compliance with the guidelines. Included were such countries as Malaysia, the Philippines, and Uruguay, which had committed to the guidelines. It also included the names of eight countries that had committed to the OECD tax haven standards but had yet to implement them—Austria, Belgium, Brunei, Chile, Guatemala, Luxembourg, Singapore, and Switzerland. Seventy countries, including Liechtenstein and Andorra, were listed as either having "substantially" implemented the proposals or having committed to them without substantial implementation. Several countries revised their policies in an effort to get their names removed from the blacklist, although some put the new policies into practice only gradually. By early 2009, only three countries remained on the blacklist.

In February 2009, Switzerland's UBS, a large bank, entered into a criminal "deferred prosecution" agreement with the US Department of Justice and was fined US$780 million for aiding and abetting tax evasion by US residents. In addition, the Swiss government agreed to deliver information on 250 UBS client accounts (furnished by UBS) to the Department of Justice, which was the first major breach of Swiss banking secrecy in broad-gauge tax matters. In the wake of that action, some UBS clients came forward voluntarily to secure more favorable treatment and avoid criminal prosecution. In August 2009, UBS agreed to turn over to the US Internal Revenue Service some 4,500 additional US client names, covering about US$18 billion in assets, without specifying the selection criteria or the timing of the disclosure.

UBS appeared to put the entire matter behind it in the intergovernmental settlement and was able to continue its rebuilding from the disaster of the global financial crisis, reputational losses, and threat of criminal sanctions. At the same time, the "easy money" of hefty charges for financial secrecy was over. For its part, the United States was unlikely to rest on its success in breaching offshore financial secrecy; other Swiss banks and other alleged financial havens were clearly on its radar screen. The Swiss government had to concede on a major point of principle and could expect to feel the heat of other governments in Europe and elsewhere seeking outcomes similar to that of the United States.

Upon the announcement of the Swiss–US agreement and the UBS settlement, a number of smaller Swiss banks, far less exposed to the United States than was UBS, were already promising more-sophisticated tax evasion schemes in the hope of attracting tax evaders in Europe and the United States. These banks included Credit Suisse, Julius Baer, Zürcher Cantonalbank, and many others that were already on the US tax authorities' radar screen. One of them, Bank Wegelin (Switzerland's oldest) was indicted on a criminal charge by the United States and soon went out of business.

In the end, a 2013 agreement allowed Swiss banks to come forward and declare that they either did or did not suspect that they had engaged in helping US residents evade taxes. Those that did suspect they were involved in tax evasion by US residents could negotiate individual penalties with the US authorities. Those that did not would have a chance to document it. The process started in 2013 and would continue until all the banks settled. But it was too late for Credit Suisse, which was forced to plead guilty to a criminal felony charge and was fined US$2.6 billion in May 2014. In the settlement process, Swiss banks were not required to reveal client identities but did have to reveal enough business information to ease the IRS's burden of tracking down the tax evaders.

Swiss banks also have to report outflows to other financial centers attractive to tax evaders, notably Singapore, and in 2015, that country reached agreement with US authorities on new aggressive measures to support US tax compliance measures. Places to hide are fewer and fewer, suggesting further shrinkage of offshore asset management pools.

Family Offices

The apex of private wealth management is arguably the "family office," which manages investment and trust assets for a single family and is staffed by professionals in various aspects of wealth management who are committed to the family's (often complex and changing) financial objectives. A variant is the multiple-family office, which serves several wealthy families in managing segregated, but sometimes pooled, investment accounts. Key issues include intergenerational wealth transfers, fiduciary obligations in trust relationships, fees paid to external asset managers, and tax efficiency. Traditional family offices may also provide such personal services as managing household staff and making travel arrangements. Other services typically handled by the traditional family office include property management, accounting and payroll functions, and management of legal affairs. Family offices often handle philanthropic activities as well.

Family offices are usually organized as independent companies with limited liability; in the United States, they have traditionally been deemed investment advisers under the Investment Advisers Act of 1940 but have relied on the "less than 15 clients" rule to avoid registration under the Act. The 2010 Dodd–Frank Act eliminated that rule, and an organized effort by single-family offices convinced Congress to exempt single-family offices that meet certain criteria from the definition of investment adviser under the 1940 Act. Consequently, family offices remain lightly regulated in comparison with hedge funds, which saw their regulatory exposure increase significantly under the Dodd–Frank Act.

For example, following an investigation for criminal insider trading, the arrest and conviction of several of its traders, and the loss of most of its institutional clients (leaving about US$9 billion of assets belonging to CEO Stephen A. Cohen and key employees), the SAC Capital Advisors hedge fund reorganized in 2014 as a family office, renamed Point72. The purpose was to avoid future reporting requirements and regulatory scrutiny.

Together with offshore wealth holdings, family offices represent one of the murkiest corners of the global asset management industry. Little reliable disclosure or credible survey data are available. Consequently, the data—starting with such basics as AUM, asset allocations, and growth—are little more than guesses by research firms and consultants.

7. Do Asset Management Firms Pose a Systemic Risk?

In the course of the 2007–08 financial crisis, the systemic risk that surfaced in connection with banks and investment banks largely bypassed asset management firms, insurance companies, and other nonbank fiduciaries. The losses that accompanied the crisis were carried by banks to the extent that they invested in the toxic asset class and by fiduciaries that passed those losses through to the accounts of the ultimate asset holders in the household section. The same was true of "waterfall" losses in other asset classes, including the stock market infected by the mortgage collapse and Great Recession that followed.

Millions of households lost trillions of dollars in savings and pension provisions, often at great personal cost, but the fiduciaries involved were not directly affected. To the extent that the asset holdings were leveraged, the owners lost even more, but the losses were widely dispersed and, in some cases, bounced back to the banks that made the loans. Again, the asset managers dodged the bullet—except for reputational losses related to bad advice and the failure to protect investor interests (and the possibility that some managers served as brokers on leveraged asset holdings).

Insurance companies, to the extent they served as fiduciaries for such products as annuities, were affected in a way similar to pension funds and other asset managers. At the same time, however, assets invested in insurance reserves, although affected, failed to trigger a liquidity crisis because clients of both nonlife and life insurance products were locked in. It also helped that the insurance firms' pure insurance businesses were tightly regulated in many jurisdictions, including the US states that are home to such major firms as MetLife and Prudential.

The one exception was AIG, which managed to have its holding company regulated by a poorly qualified agency (the Office of Thrift Supervision) and issued an enormous quantity of collateralized default swaps (CDS) through its AIG Financial Products (AIGFP) unit in London. AIG's state-regulated insurance business performed as well as its competitors through the crisis, but AIGFP collapsed, requiring a US$85 billion US Federal Reserve/Treasury bailout to avoid defaulting on its CDS and further endangering the banking system.

After the crisis, a major debate ensued about whether asset managers, insurers, and finance companies ought to be considered "systemically important" and put under Federal Reserve supervision. Such a step would involve for these institutions substantially higher capital requirements and other obligations, including stress testing. Both AIG and General Electric Capital were identified as systemically important early in the discussion. So, the debate—centering on the US Financial Stability Oversight Council (FSOC)—focused on the other large insurers, such as MetLife, and such asset managers as BlackRock, Fidelity, and Vanguard.

Insurers based their case on their inherent stability and resistance to runs, whereas asset managers based their case on the absence of exposure to client losses even under worst-case conditions. Proponents of subjecting these firms to systemic risk regulation argued that fiduciaries were so large (exceeding US$4.8 trillion in the case of BlackRock and US$3.1 trillion in the case of Vanguard) that they could "herd" in a particular direction under stressful conditions and seriously amplify financial turmoil. They further argued that large asset managers are vulnerable to "fire sales," as investors demand redemptions and head for the hills in a mass flight to quality. The industry responded that the FSOC should focus on particular financial practices that could pose systemic risks, such as leveraged exchange-traded funds. This approach would create another regulatory domain for the Securities and Exchange Commission, but it would leave even the largest asset managers and insurers relatively untouched.

In July 2015, the Financial Stability Board, comprising financial regulators from key countries/regions, decided to exempt asset managers from systemic risk regulation and, instead, focus on market liquidity—in particular, potentially toxic products and activities. So, the world's largest asset managers had dodged a bullet and escaped having to join the 30 banks and nine insurance companies on the list of "systemically important" financial institutions on a global basis and the heightened supervision, stress testing, and capital rules that come with it. Nevertheless, focusing on markets could require asset managers to hold liquidity buffers, apply "gates" to prevent redemptions in times of financial stress, and apply waiting periods before redemptions are executed.

8. Conclusion

This book has attempted to provide an overview of the global asset management industry—the buy side of global financial markets—whose core role is to gather investable funds from households, corporations, governments, and other sources so they can be deployed as efficiently as possible to end users of the funds for purposes of capital formation, consumption, and public sector expenditures. It is a fiduciary industry that carries a heavy burden in exercising duty of care and loyalty to its clients, who are exposed to agency risks in relationships with fund managers because of conflicts of interest, inefficiency, and ineptitude.

The structure of the asset management industry is highly complex in its major institutional streams: pension funds, mutual funds, hedge funds and other alternatives, and private wealth management. Each stream is itself complex, and in many cases, asset management firms must compete both within and across streams. Pension fund managers seek to attract nonpension assets. Mutual funds seek to attract defined-contribution pension assets. Mutual funds try to innovate and compete successfully with hedge funds, which in turn compete with banks in commercial lending and with private equity firms in funding new ventures and corporate takeovers. Meanwhile, virtually all asset managers, in one way or another, try to attract business from wealthy individuals and households.

Any number can play. Banks are involved in the industry through bank-owned mutual fund families, internal hedge funds, trusts, and private banking units. Broker/dealers are active in much the same way. So are such insurance companies as Prudential and TIAA-CREF. There are also stand-alone investment monolines in the United States (e.g., Fidelity, Vanguard, and BlackRock) and semi-detached asset management families (e.g., PIMCO, a subsidiary of Allianz, and Dreyfus of BNY Mellon). And there are various kinds of specialists, independent hedge funds, private equity firms, *banques privées*, trust companies, family offices, independent private bankers, and financial advisers.

What is required to excel in the industry? Significant distribution in leading markets, product breadth and consistency, global money management expertise, and capital strength lie at the core. Also needed are technological capabilities, marketing and customer service skills, defensible pricing, low-cost production, and a strong brand. All must be rooted in an affirmative culture, cohesive senior management, and a talented and motivated staff.

Despite the complexity of the business that is reflected throughout this book, the common threads that run through the discussion—growth, risk, and cost—cannot be ignored by asset managers hoping to be sustainable in the market. Sustainable competitive performance for firms in the asset management business may involve accessing sometimes unfamiliar markets to generate growth; managing all kinds of risk (market, credit, and liquidity risk as well as sovereign, operational, and reputational risk); and paying careful attention to cost control in an environment where persistent outperformance is exceedingly difficult. Still, the future looks bright. Each year, massive investable funds appear that have to be deployed in the best interests of their owners—the core mandate of this industry.

RESEARCH FOUNDATION
CONTRIBUTION FORM

☑ **Yes**, I want the Research Foundation to continue to fund innovative research that advances the investment management profession. Please accept my tax-deductible contribution at the following level:

Thought Leadership Circle.................... US$1,000,000 or more
Named Endowment .... US$100,000 to US$999,999
Research Fellow .... US$10,000 to US$99,999
Contributing Donor............................ US$1,000 to US$9,999
Friend .... Up to US$999

I would like to donate US$ _____ .

☐ My check is enclosed (payable to the CFA Institute Research Foundation).
☐ I would like to donate appreciated securities (send me information).
☐ Please charge my donation to my credit card.
         ☐ VISA   ☐ MC   ☐ Amex   ☐ Diners

Card Number

___ ___ / ___ ___   _____

Expiration Date   Name on card   P L E A S E   P R I N T
☐ Corporate Card
☐ Personal Card   _____
                               Signature

☐ This is a pledge. Please bill me for my donation of US$_____
☐ I would like recognition of my donation to be:
     ☐ Individual donation   ☐ Corporate donation   ☐ Different individual

_____
      PLEASE PRINT NAME OR COMPANY NAME AS YOU WOULD LIKE IT TO APPEAR

PLEASE PRINT   ☐ Mr. ☐ Mrs. ☐ Ms.   MEMBER NUMBER _____

_____
Last Name (Family Name)   First (Given Name)   Middle Initial

_____
Title

_____
Address

_____
City   State/Province   Country ZIP/Postal Code

Please mail this completed form with your contribution to:
The CFA Institute Research Foundation • P.O. Box 2082
Charlottesville, VA 22902-2082 USA

For more on the CFA Institute Research Foundation, please visit www.cfainstitute.org/learning/foundation/Pages/index.aspx.